FACTORS INFLUENCE FUTURE SOCIAL DEVELOPMENT

JOHN LOK

Copyright © John Lok
All Rights Reserved.

This book has been published with all efforts taken to make the material error-free after the consent of the author. However, the author and the publisher do not assume and hereby disclaim any liability to any party for any loss, damage, or disruption caused by errors or omissions, whether such errors or omissions result from negligence, accident, or any other cause.

While every effort has been made to avoid any mistake or omission, this publication is being sold on the condition and understanding that neither the author nor the publishers or printers would be liable in any manner to any person by reason of any mistake or omission in this publication or for any action taken or omitted to be taken or advice rendered or accepted on the basis of this work. For any defect in printing or binding the publishers will be liable only to replace the defective copy by another copy of this work then available.

Contents

Preface

This book explains what factors may change global human future development. in human development history, we are concerning how to create talent human from past till to nowadays. Scientists hope that human needs to be trained to be talent human from foolish human. The question is how to train or create talent human in order to reduce foolish human number in our societies. If one day, our societies can create many talent human, what influences will be brought to our future societies? What are the difficulties that we will encounter when scientists plan to train talent human? In general, human's dream is difficult to achieve because human only believes that dream is difficut to achieve. So, in general, dream is difficult to become goals to common people. Also, it can threaten anyone feels difficult to achieve our dream. In the end, general people's dreams can not implement successfully usually. Hence, usually, general people's dreams can not become any goals to implement in common.

In my this book first part , I shall find what these successful inventors, entreprensurs, country leaders and fiction writers, scientists , their same characteristics own to explain why they can succeed finally. Whether they had ever encountere unhappy or they had felt disappointed in their dream pursue journey. What do factors help them to achieve their dreams to be actual aims to implement successfully. I shall attempt to indicate the different factors to analyze why and how these factors can help them to achieve their dreams successfully finally. I hope my readers can enjoy to read this book and it can provide useful knowledge to help you to achieve your any dreams also.I shall indicate cases to explain whether scientists can achieve to create talent human aim in order to let our societies bring new exciting hope to attribute our societies. I hope that my readers can enjoy to read this book and learn new creative talent human knowledge.

Nowadays , future global job market competition will be trended serious. Any employers will expert their employees own different skills to know how to do their jobs efficiently and effectively and easily. So, future any organization employees ought considerate how to learn different kinds of skills or knowledges in order to prepare to satisfy their future employers' different new tasks needs. However, if future any new skillful needs or demands will be raised to future employers' demands. It brings these questions: what skills do global any organization employees need own in general? How to improve or raise employees themselves skills more easily and efficiently? What will happen if future employees do not learn new knowledge to improve or raise themselves skills? Why is learning any new skillful knowledge important ? What will be the possible negative and /or positive consequence if future the organizations do not need their employees to learn any new kinds of skillful knowledge?

In my this book, I shall indicate some successful people, how they own these same characteristics to achieve their unsuccessful dreams to become successful aim. I shall indicate these people how they achieve their dreams in their occupations or become business founders.The successful seeking dream people include the micro software founder " Bill Gate" explains how he pursues his computer invention dream to be succeed; the Amazon e-commerce founder , explains how he pursues his electronic commerce to achieve global online consumption leader to influence online shoppers to accept this kind of online shopping model in global; explains what are the same individual characteristics to the successful fiction authors' ; explains how any countries' president individual same characteristics; explains how scientists own same individual characteristics, e.g. internet inventor, sky scientist, they can achieve their scientific research dreams in success.

In my this book second part, I shall research how to change human have comfortable lives. Every one must need comfortable feeling to live in our earth in any country. I write this book aims to give my opinion whether what aspects are our most hope in order we can live more comfortable as well as owning safe feeling. I shall concentrate on researching these several aspects that I feel we need to concern how to improve if we hope that we can live more comfortable and satisfactory and safe in our future lives.

These several aspects that I research my include: How and why can reduce global environmental pollution to bring our advantages ? How and why can improve internet technology development to bring our advantage? How and why can improve medicine health discovery to bring our advantage? How and why can improve living environment to bring our advantage? How and why can improve social welfare to bring our advantage ?

Readers can have more clear understanding to analyze whether above these different social aspects that they will be our future main solution or improvement in order to let we can live more comfortable and safe and satisfactory in our earth.

Prologue

The differences between Asia and Western Liberal studies advantages and
disadvantages
reference
Skill training talent human method
● How to improve staff skill to be talent labour ?
p.56-76
● Career pathing strategy improve employee individual skill ?
● Strategies learning new skills

Becoming talent human encountering difficulties
● What are talent management challenges?
● Talent Management Strategy
● How to solve talent management challenges and difficulties?
Skills shortages on developing
country market
Future global skillful labor
soft knowledge skill need
2.1 Why do future labours need to
learn worldwide readiness skills
2.2 Why these occupations need
readiness skills
2.3 Data -analysis skill needs
2.4 What are regional dynamic skills
of global labour market demand
Future organizational skillful needs
how to influence workforce
change to what kinds of employees
Reference

● Individual and businessmen and governments how to improve living environment p.140-149

● reasons to improve living environment

Improving social welfare

● Why do we improve future social welfare ? p.150-159

● Can improve social welfare to influence economy growth?

Talent human development

CHAPTER ONE

IQ talent human training method

To discuss whether scientists can appy IQ method to create or train talent human. Firstly, we need to know what IQ means. According to the general consensus, the answer is "no." An IQ test measures a person's cognitive ability compared to the population at large. The average IQ is 100, anything above 130 is considered exceptionally smart while a score under 70 is categorized as developmental delays related to intelligence. An IQ test measures a person's cognitive ability compared to the population at large. The average IQ is 100, anything above 130 is considered exceptionally smart while a score under 70 is categorized as developmental delays related to intelligence. Intelligence is defined as general cognitive problem-solving skills.The equation used to calculate a person's IQ score is Mental Age / Chronological Age x 100. On most modern IQ tests, the average score will be 100 and the standard deviation of scores will be 15.

In organizational training working environment, managers across the organization are in touch with the employees you are grooming for their next big role. In larger organizations, talent management requires Human

Resources Information Systems (HRIS) that track the career paths of employees and manage available opportunities for talented employees.

● What Is Talent Management? Is talent management be IQ training method to train talent employees in any organizations?

Talent management is just another one of those pesky Human Resources terms, right? Wrong. Talent management is an organization's commitment to recruit, hire, retain, and develop the most talented and superior employees available in the job market. So, talent management is a useful term when it describes an organization's commitment to hire, manage, develop, and retain talented employees. It comprises all of the work processes and systems that are related to retaining and developing a superior workforce.

Is talent Management as a Business Strategy to any organizations ?

Talent management is a business strategy that organizations hope will enable them to retain their topmost talented and skilled employees. Just like employee involvement or employee recognition, it is the stated business strategy that will ensure the attraction of top talent in competition with other employers. When you tell a prospective employee that you are dedicated to a talent management strategy that will ensure that he or she will have the opportunity to develop professionally, you attract the best talent. This is because studies show consistently that the opportunity to continue to grow and develop their professional and personal skills is a major motivator for why employees take and stay at a job.

Differences Depending on Stated Talent Strategy

What appears to differentiate talent management focused practitioners and organizations from organizations that use terminologies such as human capital management or performance management is their focus on the manager's role, as opposed to reliance on Human Resources, for the life cycle of an employee within an organization. For example, practitioners of the other two employee development and retention strategies would argue that, for example, performance management has the same set of best practices.

Talent management does give managers a significant role and responsibility in the recruitment process and in the ongoing development of and retention of superior employees. In some organizations, only top potential employees are included in the talent management system. In other companies, every employee is included in the process. In some companies, the talent management system is accessible via computer programs; in others, informal communication among managers and HR staff is the approach used.

What Processes Are Part of a Talent Management System? You can include the following systems when you approach talent management as your overall business strategy to recruit and retain talented employees.

Recruitment planning meeting

Job description development

Job post writing and recruiting location placement for the posting

Application materials review

Phone or online screening interview

In-house interviews that can involve multiple meetings with many of your current employees

Credential review and background checking

Making the job offer to the selected person
Agreeing on the amount of the offer
Employee starting day and onboarding process
New employee welcome information and introductions
On-the-job training
Goal setting and feedback
Coaching and relationship building by the manager
Formal feedback systems such as performance management or an appraisal process
Ongoing employee development
Career planning and pathing
Promotions, lateral moves, transfers
Employment termination by choice of the employee or cause by the employer

Manager's Key Role in Talent Management

As stated, the majority of these work systems are squarely in the hands of the employee's manager. HR can provide support, training, and backup, but the day-to-day interactions that ensure the new employee's success comes from the manager. Developing and coaching the employee comes from his or her active, daily interaction with the manager.

HR can take the lead in some of the activities you see on this list, especially in recruiting and selecting new employees, and in the case of employment termination. HR is also deeply involved in the performance management system, career planning, and so forth leading the development of the systems. Hence, talent management is a business strategy and you must fully integrate it within all of the employee-related processes of the organization. Attracting and retaining talented employees in a talent management system is the job of every member of the organization, but especially managers who have reporting staff (talent). An effective strategy also involves the sharing of information about talented employees and their potential career paths across the organization. This enables various departments to identify available talent when opportunities are made or arise. On conclusion, An organization that does this kind of effective succession planning makes sure that the best talent is trained and ready to assume the next position in their career path. Succession planning benefits the employees and it benefits the organization. Managers across the organization are in touch with the employees you are grooming for their next big role. Thus, organizational talent mangement strategy may be one kind of IQ training method to raise or improve employee individual work efficiency or productive effort or creating talent skillful abilities for any organizations.

● Is An IQ Test An Accurate Way To Measure Intelligence Or Are Mental Abilities ?

The IQ test is an exam most of us are familiar with, regardless of whether we have taken it or not. The test was originally designed by the French psychologist Alfred Binet in the early 1900s. But in the new millennium, is the IQ test still an effective means of measuring general intelligence? According to the general consensus, the answer is "no." An IQ test measures a person's cognitive ability compared to the population at large. The average IQ is 100, anything above 130 is considered exceptionally smart while a score under 70 is categorized as developmental delays related to intelligence.

However, some scientists believe that intelligence is defined as general cognitive problem-solving skills. Since the days of Binet, psychologists have agreed that intelligence is much more complex than a single number and may be in fact divided into many subcategories. This is where the IQ test falls short. A Canadian study published online in the journal Neuron concluded that the IQ test is "fundamentally flawed," seeing that its questions "grossly oversimplify the abilities of the human brain." The report identified three indications of human intelligence: short term memory, reasoning skills, and verbal ability. None of these skills are at all accurately measured in the traditional IQ test. So what does the IQ test accurately measure? While the IQ test may give an indication of general intelligence, it can't measure the entire complexity of the human thought process. Creativity, emotional sensitivity, social understanding, and various acquired skills such as music or art, are excluded from test's measurements of intelligence. If you'd like to get an idea of your IQ take this test, but just remember that whatever your score be, it doesn't necessarily define how smart you really are. So, it seems that IQ test training can not guarantee to raise or improve any foolish person to be talent person in possible. So, IQ test training may not be the most suitable talent human creative method to any one. It depends on whether the suitation how to provide IQ training , e.g. organizations may attempt to apply IQ skill test method to raise or improve employee efficiency or skill to serve their organizations effectively. But, schools will be difficult to apply IQ test training method to raise student learning effort effectively.

However, I believe that IQ test training can create these kinds of talent human as below:

Your answer to that question probably depends pretty heavily on your grades in school or, if you've ever taken one, the results of an IQ test. But are those a fair basis to assess a person's mental capabilities? Everyday language suggests maybe not. We speak of street smarts and EQ, for instance. Both terms suggest that there are abilities that deserve to be considered as forms of intelligence but that fall well beyond the scope of traditional academic measures. Does science go along with common sense in seeing that intelligence and IQ are far from the same thing? More than you probably imagine. According to Harvard's Howard Gardner, intelligence actually comes in an incredible eight flavors. I shall indiate these most popular six kinds of IQ test training talent human as below:

1. Musical intelligence.

"People say, well, music is a talent. It's not an intelligence. And I say why, if you're good with words, is that an intelligence, but if you're good with tones and rhythms and timbres, it's not. And nobody's ever given me a good answer, which is why it makes sense to talk about musical intelligence.

2. Spatial intelligence.

This is the easy grasp of how things lay in space that allows a chess master to win or a surgeon to perform near miracles. It's also "what an airplane pilot or a sea captain would have. How do you find your way around large territory and large space," Gardner notes.

3. Bodily kinesthetic Intelligence.

Forget the cliché of the dumb jock. Coordinating your body actually takes a great deal of intelligence -- just not the kind measured by IQ tests. This type of smarts "comes in two flavors. One flavor is the ability to use your whole body to solve problems or to make things, and athletes and dancers would have that kind of bodily kinesthetic intelligence. But another variety is being able to use your hands or other parts of your body to solve problems or make things. A craftsperson would have bodily kinesthetic intelligence" too, according to Gardner.

4. Interpersonal intelligence.

This one seems a bit similar to the popular concept of EQ. "Interpersonal intelligence is how you understand other people, how you motivate them, how you lead them, how you work with them, how you cooperate with them," says Gardner, who adds that it's a particularly important type of intelligence for leaders to have.

5. Intrapersonal intelligence.

Intrapersonal intelligence, or self-knowledge, is both very hard to assess and very important, Gardner says, particularly in today's fast-changing world. "Nowadays, especially in developed society, people lead their own lives. We follow our own careers. We often switch careers. We don't necessarily live at home as we get older. And if you don't have a good understanding of yourself, you are in big trouble," he explains.

6. Naturalist intelligence.

This one is "the capacity to make important, relevant discriminations in the world of nature between one plant and another, between one animal and another. It's the intelligence of the naturalist, the intelligence of Charles Darwin," Gardner says. And before you argue that you live in Detroit or Manhattan and so have no need for this type of smarts, he adds that "everything we do in the commercial world uses our naturalist intelligence. Why do I buy this jacket rather than another one? This sweater rather than another one?" Those fine distinctions are made by the part of the brain that used to discern a tasty small animal from a poisonous one. "When an old use of a brain center no longer is relevant, it gets hijacked for something new. So we're all using our naturalist intelligence even if we never walk out into the woods," Gardner concludes.

The bottom line? If you've been thinking of your mental horsepower solely in terms of high school report cards or a single number from an IQ test, you're probably selling yourself short. And if you're focusing your energies only on boosting your book learning, you may be wasting efforts that could be better focused on other strengths. Hence, above six kinds of talent human ought be trained to raise skill effort on music, calculation, interpersonal communication , athletes and dancers etc. sport skill aspects. IQ test training method may be one kind of effective talent human training method choice.

● Can IQ test train talent human ?

What does science say? Is innate talent a myth? This question is the focus of the new book Peak: Secrets from the New Science of Expertise by Florida State University psychologist Anders Ericsson and science writer Robert Pool. Ericsson and Pool argue that, with the exception of height and body size, the idea that we are limited by genetic factors—innate talent—is a pernicious myth. "The belief that one's abilities are limited by one's genetically prescribed characteristics....manifests itself in all sorts of 'I can't' or 'I'm not' statements," Ericsson and Pool write. The key to extraordinary performance, they argue, is "thousands and thousands of hours of hard, focused work."

To make their case, Ericsson and Pool review evidence from a wide range of studies demonstrating the effects of training on performance. In one study, Ericsson and his late colleague William Chase found that, through over 230 hours of practice, a college student was able to increase his digit span—the number of random digits he could recall—from a normal 7 to nearly 80. In another study, the Japanese psychologist Ayako Sakakibara enrolled 24 children from a private Tokyo music school in a training program designed to train "perfect pitch"—the ability to name the pitch of a tone without hearing another tone for reference. With a trainer playing a piano, the children learned to identify chords using colored flags—for example, a red flag for CEG and a green flag for DGH. Then, the children were tested on their ability to identify the pitches of individual notes until they reached a criterion level of proficiency. By the end of the study, the children had seemed to acquire perfect pitch. Based on these findings, Ericsson and Pool conclude that the "clear implication is that perfect pitch, far from being a gift bestowed upon only a lucky few, is an ability that pretty much anyone can develop with the right exposure and training." This sort of evidence makes a compelling case for the importance of training in becoming an expert. No one becomes an expert overnight, and the effects of extended training on performance can be larger than might seem possible. But does the fact that training leads to improvements—even massive improvements—in skill level mean that innate talent is a myth? This is a much harder scientific argument to make, and is where Peak runs into trouble. Ericsson and Pool gloss over or omit critical details of research they review that undermine the anti-talent argument. As one example, although they claim that the results of Sakakibara's training study imply that "pretty much anyone" can acquire perfect pitch, the sample in that study did not include pretty much anyone. It included children who had been enrolled in a private music school from a very young age (the average age at which training began was 4). It does not seem likely that this non-random sample was representative of the general population in music aptitude or interest—factors that are known to be influenced by genetic factors. It's also not clear whether the children had acquired true perfect pitch, because there was no comparison of the children after training to people who possess this rare ability—for example, in terms of speed of identifying notes or neural correlates of performance.

As another example, describing the results of a study of ballet dancers by Ericsson and colleagues, Ericsson and Pool claim that "the only significant factor determining an individual ballet dancer's ultimate skill level was the total number of hours devoted to practice" and that there was "no sign of anyone born with the sort of talent that would make it possible to reach the upper levels of ballet without working as hard or harder than anyone else." Not mentioned is the exact magnitude of the correlation—a value of .42, where 1.0 is perfect. The fact that the correlation was modest in magnitude means that factors not measured in the study—including heritable aptitudes—could have actually accounted for more of the differences in ballet skill than deliberate practice did. As it always is in scientific debates, the devil is in the details in the debate over the origins of expertise.

Ericsson and Pool also leave out a good deal of evidence that runs counter to the anti-talent argument. For example, they claim that professional baseball players have "no better eyesight than an average person," but there is evidence to suggest otherwise. In a study published in the American Journal of Ophthalmology, Daniel Laby and colleagues assessed the vision of major and minor league baseball players in the Los Angeles Dodgers organization over the course of four spring training seasons. As David Epstein recounts in his book The Sports Gene, in the first year of the study the researchers used a standard test of visual acuity, and it turned out to be too easy. Over 80%

of the players got a perfect score of 20/15, meaning that they could see at 20 feet what an average person can see at 15 feet. In the following seasons, using a custom test, Laby and colleagues found that 77% of the 600 eyes tested had visual acuity of 20/15 or better, with a median of about 20/13. Even for young adults, this is excellent vision. Overall, Laby and colleagues concluded that "professional baseball players have excellent visual skills. Mean visual acuity, distance stereoacuity, and contrast sensitivity are significantly better than those of the general population."

Based on scientists own evaluation of the evidence, we argue in a recent Psychological Bulletin article that training is necessary to become an expert, but that genetic factors may play an important role at all levels of expertise, from beginner to elite. In other words, some people take much more training than other people to acquire a given level of skill. As it happens, Sakakibara's pitch training study provides some of the most compelling evidence of this type. There was a large amount of variability in how long it took the children to pass the test for perfect pitch—from around 2 years to 8 years. As Sakakibara notes in her article, this evidence implies that factors other than training may be involved in acquiring perfect pitch, including genetic factors. This finding is consistent with the results of recent reviews of the relationship between deliberate practice and skill, which include numerous studies Ericsson and colleagues have used to argue for the importance of deliberate practice. Regardless of domain, deliberate practice leaves a large amount of individual differences in skill unexplained, indicating that other factors contribute to expertise.

The more direct evidence for the multifactorial view of expertise comes from "genetically informative" research on skill—studies that estimate the contribution of genetic factors to variation across people in factors that may influence expert performance. In a study of over 10,000 twins, two of us found that music aptitude was substantially heritable, with genes accounting for around half of the differences across people on a test of music aptitude. As another example, in a pioneering series of studies, the Australian geneticist Kathryn North and her colleagues found a significant association between a variant of a gene (called ACTN3) expressed in fast-twitch muscle fibers and elite performance in sprinting events such as the 100 meter dash. There is no denying the importance of training for becoming an elite athlete, but this evidence (which is not discussed in Peak) provides compelling evidence that genetic factors matter, too.

On conclusion, based on this sort of evidence, many human behavioral scientists have argued that the experts are "born versus made" debate is over—or at least that it should be. There is no doubt that training is required to become an expert. Notwithstanding a report by North Korea's state-run news agency that Kim Jong-il made five holes-in-one his first time playing golf and rolled a perfect 300 his first time bowling, no one is literally born an expert. Expertise is acquired gradually, often over many years. However, as science is making increasingly clear, there is more to becoming an expert than training. Moving ahead, the goal for scientific research on expertise is to identify all of the remaining factors that matter. Hence, it seems that human behavioral scientists feel that IQ test may be one good skills to create talent skill to some kinds of humans if IQ test may prove the person has the kind of talent skill, e.g. music, sport, reading, writing, draw picture etc. art creative skills for future new creative art talent human method.

CHAPTER TWO

Educational learning training talent human method

What are the difference between TRAINING, EDUCATION, DEVELOPMENT AND LEARNING: WHAT IS THE DIFFERENCE? Employee training may be one kind of organizational training method example to any organizations, in particular, is associated with on-thejob skills acquired for a particular role, while education is seen as relating to a more formal academic background. In increasingly complex organisations, it may be argued that aspects of each are necessary to ensure full employee potential. Hence, it implies that educational learning training is not only focus to implement to school organizations . It can be applied to any organizations to train talent employees.

However, the terms training, education, development and learning may often be used interchangeably, but they can have very different, if overlapping, meanings in different contexts. In terms of human resource development, it is often necessary to define and delineate these in a bid to clarify the associated activities and desired outcomes within an organisation. Employee training, in particular, is associated with on-the-job skills acquired for a particular role, while education is seen as relating to a more formal academic background. However, in increasingly complex organisations, it may be argued that aspects of each are necessary to ensure full employee potential. For example, for human resource development, and demonstrate how they are best viewed as interconnected. So, human resource department may apply educational method to educate or training new employee individual skill in order to raise efficiency or improve performance before he/she begins to do her/his tasks for his / her department in the organization. So, education and training and development have close or interchangable relationship to be applied to improve or upgrade any new employee individual from low skill to high skill to be talent or excellent skill new employee in order to serve his/her organization efficiently.

● The best types of employee training methods for your workforce may include:
  Instructor-led training
eLearning
Simulation employee training
Hands-on training
Coaching or mentoring
Lectures
Group discussion and activities
Role-playing
Management-specific activities
Case studies or other required reading

1. Instructor-led training

Instructor-led training is the traditional type of employee training that occurs in a classroom, with a teacher presenting the material. This can be a highly effective method of employee training, especially for complex topics. Instructors can answer specific employee questions or direct them to further resources. They also allow for highly-skilled instructors to match the training level and style to the employees in the room.

However, instructor-led training does have some drawbacks, including cost and time to implement. It can also be unnecessary for concise topics. We discuss more about this in our post, "Instructor-Led Training Vs. eLearning.".

2. eLearning

eLearning, on the other hand, relies on online videos, tests, and courses to deliver employee training. Employees can do their training right in the palm of their hand with a smartphone or on their company computers.

It's one of the easiest types of employee training to roll out to larger populations, especially for employees who are remote or have high-turnover rates. With interactive games, tests, videos, activities, or even gamified components, it can also go a long way towards keeping your employees engaged with the training. Of course, eLearning also has its own challenges. Without a solid instructional design strategy behind it, the graphics and visuals that make eLearning fun can also make it gimmicky or quickly outdated. Keeping it up-to-date is also a necessary best practice. We cover the major advantages, and disadvantages, of eLearning here.

3. Simulation employee training

Simulation training is most often provided through a computer, augmented, or virtual reality device. Despite the initial costs for producing that software or technology, however, simulation training can be a necessary option for employees in riskier or high-stakes fields. You'll often see simulation training for pilots or doctors, but it can be useful for other employees too. This type of employee training is also highly-effective and reliable, allowing employees to progress consistently and at their own pace.

4. Hands-on training

Hands-on training includes any experiential training that's focused on the individual needs of the employee. It's conducted directly on the job. Hands-on training can help employees fit perfectly into their upcoming or current role, while enhancing their current skills.

A LinkedIn post notes:

"One advantage of hands-on training is that they are applicable immediately to the employees' jobs. They are also effective for training when it comes to new business equipment and procedures."

This is a time-intensive method of employee training, however, that's best used when there are enough resources available to support employees during the program. Learn more about experiential learning here.

5. Coaching or mentoring

Coaching or mentoring can share similar qualities to hands-on training, but in this type of employee training, the focus is on the relationship between an employee and a more experienced professional, such as their supervisor, a coach, or a veteran employee. The one-on-one mentoring style creates a relationship between employees that carries far beyond training. It also allows the employee to ask questions they may not feel comfortable asking in a classroom, instructor-led training. This training method can be done in person or virtually, through online coaching sessions. For all its benefits, mentoring is costly in terms of employee hours and should be used appropriately to reduce those associated costs. Coaching—bringing in a trained professional—can sometimes provide a more time-efficient alternative, but without the relationship building that's so valuable in mentoring.

6. Lecture-style training

Important for getting big chunks of information to a large employee population, lecture-style training can be an invaluable resource for communicating required information quickly. However, use this type of employee training sparingly. HR.com writes: "It has been said to be the least effective of all training methods. In many cases, lectures contain no form of interaction from the trainer to the trainee and can be quite boring. Studies show that people only retain 20 percent of what they are taught in a lecture."

7. Group discussions and activities

For the right group of employees, group discussions and activities can provide the perfect training option. It allows multiple employees to train at once, in an environment that better fits their current departments or groups. These discussions and activities can be instructor-led or facilitated by online prompts that are later reviewed by a supervisor. This type of employee training is best used for challenges that require a collaborative approach to complex issues. Find ideas for training activities here.

8. Role-playing

Similar to group discussions, role-playing specifically asks employees to work through one aspect of their jobs in a controlled scenario. They'll be asked to consider different points-of-view and think on their feet as they work through the role-playing activity. Like other group activities, role-playing is highly effective but may be unnecessary for simple, straightforward topics. It also requires more employee time, potentially taking time away from an entire department while they're going through the training.

9. Management-specific activities

Management-specific activities are just that—employee training that's focused on the needs of managers. They may include simulations, brainstorming activities, team-building exercises, role-playing, or focused eLearning on management best practices. While management training can include many different types of training, it's important to consider the additional needs of your managers separately from the rest of your employee population. This ensures they have the foundation they need to support the rest of their staff.

10. Case studies or other required reading

Finally, some employee training topics are readily accessible through required readings. Case studies, in particular, can provide a quick way for employees to learn about real workplace issues. Employees can read through these at their own pace, or while working in a team-building session with other employees. Case studies are a great option for focused topics, but more complex topics will likely require more advanced types of employee training.

All of above these education or training methods may be any schools or organizations may choose to apply in order to teach their employees or students to learn effectively.

● What is Talent oriented education to human development?

One lesson is that talent-oriented education builds a strong sense of self-efficacy, effective goal setting, and a personal commitment that can enhance students' specific achievements and lead them to higher-level career accomplishments. Others favoring the establishing of a talent development group in their organizations believe the term will help promote training. As one participant noted, "It helps with the marketing of 'training' itself. Everyone needs the basic training when they enter an organization, but they need to continue learning. To continue the training, through the concept of developing an employee's talent, goes a long way toward reception and retention." Still others favoring the establishment of a talent development group see the primary value as motivational. For Role Of Education In Human Development example, Education gives the ability to think with reason, pursue dreams and aspirations in life and live a respectable life in the society. Education gives us a definite path to follow, to lead our lives by principles and gives us the freedom of expression. It frees our minds from the prejudices and motivates it to think with logic and reason. It is essential for the overall development of the human mind and brain. The literacy rate of a country determines its prosperity and economic health.The benefits of education are numerous, but a few points are highlighted below, which shows how education helps in human development from different aspects – personal, social, economic and spiritual.

In fact, every human has dreams and aspirations. So, education is a medium to pursue and fulfill them. It increases the knowledge of a person in different fields of studies. It helps to determine a path to follow and express your talent to the world.

Enhance creativity and imagination: Education opens up

new ways and ideas to ponder. It cultivates a young mind to think out-of-the-box and explore different things in life. Education also helps to know about things and stay healthy, fit and follow a productive lifestyle.

Education is a way of academic excellence and paves the path for economic growth of the country. Research and development in sectors like technology, medicine, and others, breakthrough innovation and progressive mindset – all of this are fruits of education, which takes a nation and its people forward. Educated people contribute towards advancement in every sector. Education opens up every channel of knowledge and wisdom. It exposes us to a whole new world of information, invent new things and know how we can make our surroundings a better place to live and out our lives to a greater, and better use. Education can train any poor knowledge students to learn new knowledge or poor skillful staffs learn new job knowledge for organizations. So, education is one kind of new learning method to train poor or foolish knowledge student to be clever or poor performance staff to be clever or talent staff both in schools or business organizations.

● Behavioral economic solves classroom management discipline

How to apply behavioral economic method to help teachers to solve classroom management discipline in order to raise student individual learning interest in classrooms? Students need to know what classroom management means. It means effective discipline, it is being prepared to motivate students to raise interesting to learn in classrooms. It is providing a safe, comfortable learning environment, it can build the teacher individual student's sale esteem and creative and imaginative in daily lessons.

Why has classroom management relationship to student individual behavior as well as why behavioral economic method can be applied to solve classroom management discipline in possible? It is simple because every teacher teaching styles, personality attitudes and every teacher management strategies are different and are not effective. It is possible that due to teaching experiences. Student population to every lesson, low or high salary level, every teacher individual time preparation and time management factors. Then all issues concern whether every teacher to do choice to arrange whose time to prepare before he/she will teach which lesson on that day. For example, if the teacher feels tried to teach more than fine lessons on that day, because he/she is sick. But the school has no enough teachers number to replace the student to teach his/her students on that day. So, he/her teaching performance can not b better , satisfaction and enjoyment in teaching are dependent upon how he/she leads students to cooperate.

Hence, he/she can not permit to so personal rest behavioral choice, and he/she feels that salary can not be raised to double payment or more to get overtime allowance on that teaching day. It will bring any unsatisfactory and unenjoyable teaching attitude or poor teaching behavior or performance and teacher won't deal with discruptive behaviors. Buy, also manage to minimize off task, non-disruptive teaching behavior to teach students and manage their own behavior to learn in classroom effectively and efficiently. Their poor classroom management behavior will bring poor teaching performance. Hence, students won't feel the school teachers are good teachers and students' families will lose confidence to let the school teachers to teach their students.

In Behavioral economic teaching method view point, the school needs to review whether its teachers number is enough to prepare some teachers need to rest at home suddenly. So, other teachers can replace them to teach any his/her lessons on that day immediately. If the school neglected to employ extra enough part time teachers number to prepare to replace any full time teachers who have need to rest on any days. Due to salary expenditure increasing reason, it is not good choice to reduce to employ extra part time teachers number to avoid the sudden full time teachers number shortage need. It will bring classroom management changes poor, due to unsatisfactory teachers' teaching need to go to classroom to teach their students in classrooms when they are sickness on that teaching day suddenly. Therefore, poor teaching performance or poor classroom management behaviors to the teacher which will bring poor economic loss, e.g. student enrollment number reduces, students absent number to every lesson increases school teaching subjects number decreases too the school in long time.

Therefore, all these poor influences will cause the school's economic loss, it is due to the school teachers' teaching behaviors are poor , due to many teachers do not enjoy and feel satisfactory to teach these students and manage classes disciplines effectively. It seems that whether the school has enough teachers number, it can influence how teacher individual teaching and class management behavior to be better or worse and then which will have relationship to influence the school's economic gain or loss in long term consequently.

Therefore, in teacher individual behavioral psychological view point, every one ought have effective time allocation method to prepare how to teach whose students in every lesson. I shall recommend how the teacher individual behavioral economic choice to solve discipline challenges in classrooms as below:

1. Transitions vs. allocated time method

The school teachers can allocate time periods they intend for their students to be engaged in learning activities as well as they can arrange transition time allocated for learning activities. For example, getting students assembled and attentive, assigning reading and directing to begin, getting students' attention away from reading and preparing for class discussion in their schools.

The transition is allocated time to teacher individual behavioral goal is to increase the variety of learning activities , but to decrease transition time, student engagement and non-task behaviors are dependent on how smoothly and efficiently to teachers more from one learning activity to another.

Therefore, teacher has witness if when classroom discipline problems occur, the teacher consistently takes action to solve the misbehavior of exactly those students who do in classrooms, when two discipline problems arise as the same time, the teacher can deal with the more serious first. The teacher can decisively handle instances of off- task behavior before the behaviors either set out of hand or are modeled by others. When handling misbehavior makes sure all students learn what is unacceptable about that behavior, deal with misbehavior without disrupting the learning activity.

2. Classroom rules for student individual behavioral conduct. Formalized statements that provide students with general guidelines for the types of behaviors that are require and the types that are prohibited a few rules are easier to remember than many rules, each rule in a small

set of rules is more important than each rule in a large set of rules.

Why do need necessary classroom rules of conduct? It aims to maximize on -task behaviors and minimize off-task (discuptive) behaviors, secures the safety and comfort of the learning environment, prevents the activities of the class from disturbing other classes, establish an learning environment in which achieving specified learning goals takes priority over other concerns in classrooms, be particularly prepared and organized to minimize transition time and utilizes a communication style that establishing non-threatening, comfortable environment to let students to learn in classrooms. Other components of disclosure statement include: basis course outline, grading procedures, include procedures for making up missed work, extra credit homework expected etc., attendance policies should be consistent with school policy, other class rules, policies procedures, safety considerations as necessary , accommodation for disabilities statement, signature of student and parent / guardian. Therefore, classroom rules can influence how student individual chooses to do whose learning conduct or behavior , even improving their learning attitude in classrooms. Classroom rules are the best method to influence every student how to choose to do whose learning behaviors in classroom in order to earn the most effective learning benefits for themselves.

Finally, I shall discuss how to apply behavioral economic method to raise student learning interest at classrooms? As I explained that when teacher feels that individual satisfactory or enjoyable teaching feeling to do his/her teaching job, which will influence whose teaching performance in classrooms. Thus, how to improve every teacher individual teaching performance or method or teaching quality which will be important factor to influence whose student individual learning interest to be raised in classrooms indirectly.

I recommend that teachers need to concern how to arrange classroom teaching environment to be attractive or safe or enjoyable to influence every student individual learning attitude to increase more attention or concentrate to hear whose teacher's teaching to his/her any lessons in the classroom more considerately. Arrangement is determined by learning activity (lecture, class discussion, small group work etc. learning activities in classrooms). Thinking thorough class procedure and learning activities and arrangement the classroom in the best possible way.

Teachers need to know why the student chooses to do his/her behavior in classroom. Usually, every behavior has a function , three primary reasons for disputive behavior in the classroom include power, attention, what to be left alone (i.e. disinterest or feelings of inadequacy). Many misbehavior are exhibited by students are responses to a behavior needs exhibited by the teacher to understand why a person exhibits behavior is no reason to tolerate it, teacher needs to understand the function of a behavior will help in knowing how to deal with that behavior. When, the teacher can understand why the student chooses to do his/ her behavior to find the solutions to persuade or dissuade the student does not choose to do the harmful behavior or change the harmful behavior to do right behavior in order to influence other students can not concentrate on learning considerately.

Consequently, if the school expected to raise every student individual learning interest in classrooms. The school needs to find methods to let its teachers feel satisfactory to teach their students in the school as well as the school's teachers need to learn how to understand why the student chooses to do harmful behavior to influence other students concentrate on easier learning in an enjoyable learning classroom environment.

When the school can let its teachers to enjoy to do their teaching jobs and they can feel more satisfactory when they are teaching every time in classroom as well as its teachers can understand some students why they choose to do harmful learning behavior to influence the other students to concentrate on learning in classrooms and they can find the solvable methods to dissuade they do not choose to do harmful learning behavior to influence other students can not concentrate on learning in classrooms again. Then, between the school's teachers and students both can build positive teaching attitudes and learning attitudes in order to cause they can choose to do enjoyable and satisfactory teaching behaviors or performances to teacher and concentration on learning behavior or attitudes to students in classrooms.

Consequently, when the school can build a good classroom learning environment to let teachers consider to teach their students in order to bring whose students can concentrate on learning in classrooms. Then, a good classroom learning environment will bring good learning economic and non-economic benefit , such as student number increases , school income increases and teachers salaries increase, student individual attention will raise, student will enjoy to go to school and absence number will reduce. Consequently, any schools' teacher individual teaching behavior and student individual learning behavior both in classrooms which must have positive or negative relationship to bring the school itself and the teachers themselves long term economic and non-economic benefits in learning behavioral economic view point. Also, the importance is that learning behavioral economic analysis, can explain why the teacher individual good or bad emotion can influence his/her every lesson student individual learning emotion to be good or bad to do learning behavior in clasaroom. So, schools need to concern every teacher individual emotion whether he/she feels enjoyable or satisfactory to teach his/her students in classrooms in order to avoid every classroom students' learning emotion will be influenced to be poor to bring long time economic loss to the school. It is one important factor to influence any school's teaching performance to be succeed.

Successful persuasive teaching method can raise student individual
learning behavior

Can teachers apply behavioral economic method to raise student individual learning behavior? Behavioral economic method is explained by psychology and other disciplines to create models of limits on rationality, willpower and self-interest. Although, economic professionals believe it can be applied to predict consumer behavior. But, how any why can it be applied to raise student personal interest to learn new knowledge in education industry aspect? This is one valuable research question. If it can be applied to educational psychology aspect to raise student individual learning interesting influentially, educators ought need to learn to how to do in order to persuade student individual has more interest to learn in anywhere schools or homes or libraries in habitually persuasively. I shall explain some possible educational psychological methods as below:

When one student discovered that learning will bring much tangible and intangible benefits to influence his/her career development in the future. For example, he/she can find good jobs, earn more salaries, raise the high class social positon, build personal successful image or raise satisfactory feeling, raise social competitive effort in job market etc. different economic related benefits or non economic related benefits both. Then, the teacher or the school will have possible to persuade whose students to raise learning interest when they choose to learn in the school.

How to let the student to feel the school can give good economic related or non-economic related benefits to satisfy the student future career plan successful development need persuasively and attractively? It will need to include psychological factor to influence its students to raise learning interest when they are studying in the school in whose learning experience stage. I assume that every student will learn hardly when the school can persuade its students can believe that they must earn good career benefit when they can follow the school's discipline to learn hardly in whose whole learning stage in the school.

Therefore, one successful persuasive teaching method can influence or persuade the students choose to learn hardly . Usually, in general students need not expect to waste learning time and money to chose one poor teaching quality of school to study. If they can not achieve good examination results or they need increase long time to extend their graduation time, then they will feel waste money and time loss to choose the wrong or unsuitable school to study. It is one rational either positive or negative learning feeling when one student gain good or bad examination result consequently.

Hence, one successful school must let students to have confidence , it can raise good quality teaching method to let them to study as well as it can provide good learning environment to let them to feel safe, enjoyable , attractive , persuasive learning attitude when they go to school to enter the classroom to learn every day. So, the school must need to let all students to feel they won't waste money and time economic or non-economic related losses when they choose the school to learn, if the school expected to persuade its students to choose to learn easily.

Therefore, learning behavioral economic theory explains that student individual learning interest whether whose interest is raised or not which has been related to influence whether he/she feels his/her learning attitude or learning behavior will bring either waste learning time and money loss or not in whole learning career in the school consequently. Usually, every student won't expect to waste his/her learning time and money if he/she can not earn economic or non-economic related benefits to his/her future job career.

It implies that non-wasted time and money psychological factor brings to the student feeling to learn that will be one man economic factor to influence the student chooses to do hard learning behavior. For example, when a young age student does not choose to go to the school, because he/she does not concern whether he/she will earn a better life in the future. He/she must be persuaded to feel the school is fun now or is given no better opinion to compare the school. Hence, the school needs to let the young age student to feel there are not other schools opinions are better to compare to the school as well as the school can provide attractive teaching method to let the student to feel more fun to learn when he/she chooses the school to learn.

Therefore, providing fun learning environment and fun teaching method both factors will be one important to encourage the student to learn hardly. The particular educational outcomes worth encouragement, such as attainment, attendance, and homework issues of these educational components will must be achieved fun learning feeling to let the student to whose learning interest encouragingly or persuasively. So, fun learning environment can bring the student individual learning interest in possible. It means that if the student does not feel fun to learn when he/she goes to the school to learn every day. Then, he/her poor fun learning feeling will discourage he/she feels why he/she needs to go to school to attend every lesson to learn in classrooms hardly. So, fun learning environment. fun teaching method, fun homework, fun learning content etc. teaching related components factor will encourage every student likes to go to school to listen every lesson hardly every day in possible. Present-biased learning behavior has important implications in education. Doing fun home works, studying for fun exams, researching fun colleges or potential opportunities for financial aid and completing applications all involve educational cost which will let any students choose to weigh the future learning cost to evaluate which school will be possible to bring educational loss spending cost to evaluate whether he/she ought to choose which school to study in preference. Hence, it explains that the student will consider whether the school can provide fun learning environment and fun learning subjects or courses to let them to choose to study and whether he/she can feel fun teaching method to satisfy whose learning need. Then, the school will be possible increased successfully chance to let the student to choose it to enroll to study in preference. Moreover, attractive courses choices, providing fun learning environment, providing good and fun teaching method quality , fun teaching book contents choices to let students to study etc. these factors will encourage students to raise learning interest successfully.

However, any schools need focus only on salient factors , it implies that even simple optimizing decisions may not always be made. So, with a better understanding of student individual fun learning environment and fun teaching method learning need and fun courses teaching learning contents , subjects choices etc. these factors will possible bring knowledge to design more effective learning policies and improve student individual learning outcomes.

Moreover, improving student learning attitude factor is also important to raise whose learning interest. For example, by reading motivational passages or watching movies which can encourage students to focus on positive identifies related to learning and intellectual curiosity may be one approach a growing evidence suggests that many students and parents are not fully informed about education costs , future economic and non-economic related benefits and options. It is possible related to whose low-income family backgrounds and poor learning attitude both factors. So, if the family was one high income family, it will have possible to influence whose sons or daughter to build good learning attitude. When they have good learning attitude and good family growing relationship . The, they will raise learning interest , due to they had built from good learning attitude when they are living in one good family relationship environment. In special, when the family is one low income family and low educational level background, parents will been to work, so they will neglect to teach whose sons or daughters to know whether they ought how to learn easily, which will be one correct or right learning attitude to learn by themselves successfully. They will neglect and lack useful educational recommendation to compare education cost, future economic and non-economic educational benefits and learning attitude and opinion methods and the suitable courses and teaching books contents opinions to let whose their sons and/or daughters to know how to learn effectively by themselves, instead of school teaching method. So, these students' parents' lacking useful learning recommendation or negligent education learning recommendation behaviors which will also cause the low income family students to build " discouraged hard learning attitude" to let them to raise interest to learn any more new knowledge persuasively. Even, due to the non-educational behavioral opinion of pre-school decision making opinion, if the parents discovered that the school is one suitable school to let their sons and/or daughters to learn persuasively or attractively in order to let they can earn good examination results or pass subjects more easily. Then, these disappointed parents and low grade examination result of students will feel need to learn more hardly if they are still not improving their grade when they feel that they had been studying hardly in the school. Consequently, it will bring more negative learning emotion to the students and families. Hence, disappointing or poor or negative learning attitude or emotion to the student's feeling , this factor must not raise the student individual interest to learn in the school. Otherwise, positive or good learning emotion or attitude will influence the student to raise learning interest to continue to learn in the school consequently. hence, schools ought not neglect to improve students to build positive learning emotion or attitude habitually in order to raise whose interest to learn in the school more easily.

Can effective school management behavior raise student learning interest

How and why effective school management behavior can influence the school's student individual to raise learning interest. What is the relationship to bring student individual learning interest to be raised between the student and the school? An effective school management behavior can make the function bring that teaching and learning take place in the most effective way. In managing school's systems have to operate so that a whole range of social, intellectual and emotional activities can evolve and develop (pay foot et , 1989). It seems that an effective school management system can change student individual to do a range of positive social, intellectual and emotion activities in order to raise whose learning interest.

Therefore, innovating the traditional education system, changing many aspects of school structures, systems and organization as well as recognizing that the more teachers at all levels in a school's hierarchy who had management training of some kind, the better is needed to some traditional educational organizations. Any educational organizations need have good management functions ,which include: setting the right aims and objectives, planning how a goal will be achieved, organizing available educational resources (how teaching time arrangement, how to select teachers and clerical staffs, homework, how revision time allocation, how educational material opinions, e.g. computers facilities, classrooms number and design method and teaching environment, lecture hall seats number, tables and chairs number, library teaching book lending supplies number etc. resources arrangement) . Therefore, the school can be economically achieved in a planned way, controlling the teaching process (i.e. ensuring that the goal is achieved, e.g. raising learning interest to every individual student when he/she is learning at classrooms, reducing the students fail exam and/or test result number.

In fact, if the school expects it can be one real teaching organization, if the school can arrange internal and external structures effectively. Then, the school let students to have more confidence to choose the school to study. Internal structures include: class organizing, subject choice organization, departments organizing, responsibility arranging. Otherwise , external structures include: admission numbers, numbers on raising salary scales, school budget, leaving ages, holiday length of the school day, arrangement methods of appraisal etc. Hence effective school management system can bring more confidence to the student to choose to the school to study and it can encourage him/her to raise learning interest effectively.

So, it seems that student learning interest has close relationship to concern how the school manages its organization. Because good school management can influence its internal and external teaching resources how to allocate to use and manage effectively. For example, good classroom teaching environment can influence students to feel easily, an teaching book library can have enough different topic teaching book to let students to borrow to read, or it has enough commuter facilities to let students to find any reading data from internet conveniently. Then , they will be influenced to raise learning interest more easily, because the school has one attractive and fun learning environment to let its students to learn.

Therefore, an effective school management system can influence its students to raise more interest to learn in order to influence they choose to do learning behavior to study more harder in homes or schools. How to bring one effective school management system to influence students to feel? I shall indicate the main factors as below:

The first factor is one effective school management system needs have an effective hierarchy of head teachers, deputy heads, heads of department different effective organizing systems. It aims to achieve more directing, controlling and commanding to any department leaders to manage themselves departments more easily.

One educational organization's hierarchical pyramid can indicate such as: a head teacher manage or leads one deputy or more than one deputies on the top level, the middle level will include one deputy or more than one deputy manager(s) or lead(s) in one department head or more than one department heads. Next, the middle level will include one department head or leads more than one teacher at the low level. However, any school organization expects to manage or lead themselves schools effectively. They need to organize in such a way that they will try to achieve effective results and make every effort to maintain good relationships between those who work in these departments.

Consequently, when the school can have effective hierarchical structure to manage all different teaching staffs to do whose individual teaching behavior effectively. Then, it will bring positive emotion influence to every teacher to teach whose students more effectively. Hence, every classroom students' learning attitude will enjoy to bring more learning feeling when they are real raised learning interest from their teachers' teaching method influence persuasively.

The second factor is that each staff group participation. It will be the school's staff group participation behavioral factor, how it influences every classroom overall students' learning behaviors to be positive learning emotion or attitude when they (every classroom overall students) are listening their every teacher individual teaching in every lesson in every the classroom. It is important to find out who participates a lot and why, as well as why someone, e.g. teacher contributes every little to the classroom students. For example, it is because of fear, disagreement or disinterest, the group of teachers may under have useful point to make. So, a group should ideally encourage all its participates to contribute to any discussions and decision making. This issue of participation is one that group leaders have to consider very carefully.

In fact, influence and participation to every teaching group are not always the same. Some teaching staffs who tell a lot may not always be listen to . Others who are quiet and speak very little can, when they do speak, capture, the attention of everyone. If this is the case then whoever participates may alter and change depending on who has influence at a specific time and who needs certain individuals to speak and support his or her particular cause. The final factor is that the school needs to know how the styles to be influenced to every teaching group. Influence can take may forms, it can be both positive and negative. It can either to support or co-operation of others or refuse or nor support or co-operation of others. How this happen with a teaching group can be autocratic teaching colleagues who will attempt to impose their will on the teaching group by movement towards directions in which they eagerly support everyone and everything and try to avoid conflict at any cost and those who is influenced by distancing themselves from the whose proceeding influence others to do the same. Hence, in a effective teaching group , the teacher's header, e.g. deputy or head teacher ,the middle level staffs or the top level staffs will need to manage themselves every teaching group, e.g. each classroom teacher individual teaching behavior is more easily and effectively. When the classroom teacher can have good teaching performance to teach his/her students in the lesson. Then, he/she can raise every lesson's student individual learning interest more easily or persuasively.

The final school management factor is that, what is the most suitable or right school ethos and whose school aims to the school. If the school chose the most right school aims, then it can able to develop attitudes which won't only help pupils to learn more effectively or raise their interest to learn only, even , it can shoe them the technique of learning and how to continue to want to learn. I shall recommendation that these characteristics of the most suitable or right school aims in order to achieve effectiveness and a positive ethos the following characteristics will help as below:

An effective and powerful leadership, the deputy head needs to be involved in all major decisions, all teachers need to feel that they own those decisions that directly affect them, there to be consistency and continuity throughout the school organization, e.g. in terms of discipline, patterns, homework number and course content test or examination questions contents allocation policies, resource management, subject courses timetable structures etc. teaching sessions need to be structures, matched to pupils' needs, the actual teaching should be intellectually challenging for all pupils, the learning environment of the school whether it will be task -and -work orientated, i.e. every pupil will recognize learning is the norm rather than the exception, there will be lots of communication between teachers and pupils both inside and outside the classroom, record-keeping and assessment are sensible and thorough and are communicated to parents when necessary in a way that they can understand, whether there is a positive learning climate where emphasis is placed on praise rather then criticism control in classrooms is firm , but fair, with children being treated as individuals, any teaching or resource allocation , teaching time allocation activities whether are organized to take place outside the classroom and away from the school. This is a means of offering pupils wider experiences and a way of putting. The academic content of the curriculum into a different content.

Consequently, how to organize the school in effective way factor which will be one main influential factor to influence teachers to do positive or negative teaching behavior to persuade whose students can raise more learning interest in classrooms. So, it seems that teacher individual positive or negative teaching emotion or attitude will influence their teaching performance or teaching behavior to improve to be better in order to raise the school's students' learning interest more easily or persuasively.

Raising student learning effort reasons, influences
and benefits

Why do schools need to learn how to raise students learning effort? If schools do not consider to raise studnts effort, what negative influences to schools and students and parents will encounter. How to persuade students to learn the skills to raise whose reading ability more easily? Why should schools and students need to pursue learning and teaching targets? How can schools raise student achievement if schools feel they need to implement strategies to raise students learning effort? I believe schools have responsbilities to help students for understanding every lessom more easily.

● What reasons that teachers and school leaders need to consider how to raise students learning efforts

Nowadays, teachers have responsibilities to design the right learning target for todays lesson. However, the right learning target for today's lesson builds on the learning targets from previous lessons in the unit and connects with learning targets in future lessons to raise student understanding of important concepts and skills. So, it brings the reason why teachers need to consider how to raise students learning efforts. The reason is because today lessons' educational quality or teacher individual teaching performance experts to improve, it needs to achieve the right learning target for today's lesson from previous lessons that the teacher's teaching experience in the unit and connects with learning target in future lessons to raise studnt understanding of important concepts and skills. Due to this reasons, if the teachers expected whose students can understand concepts and skills more easily. He/she must need to let whose students to learn how to raise whose learning effort in the beginning.

Moreover, another reason why teachers need to learn how to raise students, learning effort is that to let students to increase understanding and skills and produce strong evidence of their learning. In some educators' teaching experience shoule that adopting a learning target of the action , such as re-examine the fundamentals of teaching and learning that positively and powerfully. Hence, it seems any lesson teaching and learning successful teachers and schools and students must need to consider how to improve students learning efforts.

What is learning target theory of action? The most effective teaching and the most meaningful student learning happens when teachers design the right learning target for today's lesson and use it along with their students to aim for and assess understanding. Another reason is that teachers can be trained to learn how to do any future decision making more easily. If they expected to be one decision making expertise. So, when they can be trained to learn how to implement the best solution methods to solve any chanllenges in the short time. Then, they can be trained to make the most accurate solution methods to raise whose students' learning effort in order to let students feel more satisfactory for their teaching efforts. In the raising teachers' teaching effort if teachers expected to become better able to implement any solution methods to improve students learning efforts. They can attract to plan and implement effective instruction, describe exactly what students will learn , how well they will learn it, what they will do to demonstrate that learning, using their knowledge of typical and not so typical student progress to increase student understanding, establishing teacher look-for to guide instructional decisions, and translating success criteria to studnt look-for that promote the development of assessment- capable students.

The another reason is that parents are usually considerate their sons or daughts their examination results. So, the effect of raising students' learning efforts that will be parents and student voice. Teachers need to improve students learning efforts in order to raise individual teaching ability and improve teaching performance to satisfy parents and childrens' learning need.

● What are the influences if the school teachers and leaders do not consider how to raise students' learning effort?

When the school does not consider how to raise students' learning effort, then it will bring negative or bad students' voice effort to influence public feels it is not one successful teaching school. As (Fielding, 2006) indicated that through student voice efforts, open conversation about injustices in schools can be held.

These conservations results in equity issues that the administrators would naturally shy way from being discussed . As such, including student voices into school reforms has the advantage of broadening the conversation that adults typically have when they are engaging in school reform effort. Hence, when the school can let parents feel their daughts or sons their examination results are improved as well as the students feel themselves examination results are also improved . Then, they will have good voice to help the school to advertise or promote its successful teaching image to let public people know. It will bring positive or good influence to keep the schools' competitive effort and attract many students to choose it to study and it also reflect the school.

Warren (2005) also showed that relationship power acknowledges that effective learning can only take place in an environment of trust and cooperation. In such an environment, students are more motivated to learn and to achieve the academic objectives that have been not for them. Hence, it also meand that the school's raising students' learning efforts in success. It can influence the students' parents and students themselves believe it has the best learning environment and the school employs th most excellent teachers indiviual teaching methods and teaching experience and teaching ability to teach whose students.

In long term influence, students will be encourage more motivated to learn and to improve to achieve the academic objectives by the effective learning environment of trust and cooperation psychological factor. So, when many students can improve academic results, it will influencee their learning efforts to be raised and it will cause they will believe it has good teaching and learning reform policy.

Then, it will bring positive influence about self-evaluation on the part of the teacher which has the potential of producing changes in teaching practices of producing changes in teaching practices that are not productive. It also influence that the input from students helps teachers to develop a more clear and easily understanding complete picture of the needs of the students and the kind of classroom strategies choice easily that the best support raising student learning and eventually academic in long term success.

The most important influence is that every teacher will efforts whethet their raising student lerning efforts aim can be achieved in success, when every students themselves and parents' voice or feedback is positive or negative to let them to feel when they achieve any strategies to attempt to raise every student's learning effort for a long time, e.g. three months, six months, nine months , even one year. It can ask questionnaires to enquire their response to know whether their emotions are satisfactory or dissatisfactory to its teachers' performances in order to evaluate every teacher's teaching ability to decide their next year salary range evaluation, even it can gather every class students' ideas to know whether any subjects of th teacher individual teaching method or skill or knowledge, whose aspects will be whose weakness(es) in order to concentrate on focusing to review his/her weakness(es) and achieve the improvement of his/her teaching effort intention.

As Adonis and Macayan (2011) demonstrate that the teaching method employed by individual teachers has a huge impact on the learning outcomes of the students. Most teachers are inclined to engage in one particular teaching style which they perceive to be most effective. This assumption by the teacher on what is the best teaching method for the studens may be wrong (Seale, 2010).

Students voice has he ability to provide feedback that can be used to enhance the learning environment. Literature suggests that the most important aspect of gathering student feedback on classroom practices is responding to it (Cook-Sather, 2009; Cook-Sather, 2002; Lewis, 2001) that it ought know how to let the teacher to review its weakness(es) or improve teaching performance or teaching methods to teach every particular subject more clearly.

● Raising learning efforts benefits to schools and students and parents

What benefits will bring to the school, its students and its studnts' parents if the school achieved any successful teaching methods or strategies to be attempted to rise its poor students' learning efforts? I shall indicate some actual benefits as below:

The first benefit will be brought to impact of professional learning communities on teaching practice and student learning hand, due to the complexities of teaching and learning within a climate of increasing accountability, this raising students learning efforts reform will push professional teaching development beyond supporting the acqusition of new teaching knowledge and skills for teacher needs. Hence this new raising student learning efforts to student learning reform requires most teachers to rethink their own teaching practice to construct new classroom roles and expectations about student outcomes , such as achievement to raise student learning efforts, and to teach in ways they have never taught before, such as finding the most suitable or useful teaching methods or teaching strategies or teachin skills to raise the school students learning effort.

Thus, in the progress of the teacher attempts to find whose teaching weakness(es) is (are) and review his /her teaching weakness(es) and she /she also needs to find the most suitable or useful teaching methods or teaching skills or teaching strategies to teacher his / her students in order to raise his / her students learning efforts in the school. When, he / she tells the fail examination result of student number is increasing to any subjects, it implies that he / she has responsibilty to change his / her teaching method to adopt another kind of teaching method to attempt to teach his / her students for the subject(s). It aims to increase the pass examination results of student number to the failure subject(s). So, it will bring the school's students have chance to experience learning and learn another new kind of studying method or studying skills to replace the traditional studying method.

The teacher has also chance to experience the new teaching method experiment to find whether the new teaching method is suitable to be adapted to the school's students learning. Thus, it brings the raising students learning effort experiment benefit, it gives new teaching practice change chance as a result of participation in a improving studnts learning effort or supporting increased student learning effort strategy implement between the school's teacher and his / her students.

Why does every school need to consider how to raise students learning effort issue. It is grounded into two assumptions. First , it is assumed that knowledge is situated in the day-to-day lived experiences of teachers and best undestand through critical reflection with others who share the same experience (Buysse, Sparkman, & Wesley, 2003). Second , it is assumed that actively engaging teachers in raising students learning effort im, which will increase their professional teaching method knowledge and enhance student learning.

Consequently, in an educational climate that is increasingly directed by the demands of the poor learning effort students and their parents both. It is only the choice of the best or the most useful or the most suitable teaching method, the viability will be determined by the school and teachers and students succes in enhancing the school's student achievement. This makes it educators to demonstrate how their teaching work in raising student learning effort in order to improve student learning long term benefits.

The second benefit considers to train students' intelligence to be improved. In psychological view point, when the school attempt to find the most suitable teaching method(s) to improve the poor learning effort of students' reading abilities or studying abilities. Then, it will bring long tem intelligence benefits to the poor learning effort students to be improved. It is benefits to the student personal development in learning career.

Then, it supposes that if the poor learning effort student feels whose reading or studying ability is improved. Then, it will encourage the student accept to spend more extra time to concentrate in caring about and investing themselves in learning. So, the student fosters motivation, increased learning effort, willingness to t

take or new challenges, greater self-confidence, and a higher level of success.

Hence, raising student learning effort strategies or methods can help students to raise intelligence study skills, time management and memory strategies. In addition, the poor learning effort students can take chance to be trained or experiment about how intelligence develops. Some educators indicated that the more they exercise it , the stronger it becomes. They learned that every time, they try hard and learn something new, their brain form new connections that over time, make them smarter. They learned that intellectual development is not the natural intelligence, but rather than information of new connections brought about through effort and learning.

Moreover, when teachers find whether which kinds of learning method(s) or skill(s) or strategy (strategies) is (are) the most suitable or useful the best to raise the learning effort students in the classroom in the student learning effort research procdure. Teacher and students both also earn these benefits, such as they are noticed a marked improvement in the motivation and effort of the poor learning effort students group in the classroom. In the past, the student thought that he / she had poor learning effort to do any homework and put in minimal effort beforehand, but if the student feels him / her learning effort to be improved. Then, he / she will have much confidence to work for hours finish any assignment early. When he / she got feedbaack from his / her teacher's revist it and if he /she could earn higher grade.

Overall, the achievement of the poor learning effort students' any assignments or examinations grade raising which will bring the benefits, such as the growth mind-set changes that perspective and makes school a place where studetns engage in the high or low learning effort students learning for their own benefits. Instead , educators can help them gain the tools , they need to maintain their confidence in learning by keeping them focused on the process of achievement.

The third benefit indicates schools raising students effort strategy, which can influence on students further learning development for long term. Schooling has direct effects on every student's educational achievement, their acquisition of literacy, numeracy and scientific knowledge particular and specific skill aspects. These basic skills provide the foundation for later subjects, such as geography, psysics and foreign languages (Good & Brophy, 1986 b) showed that the learning of specific knowledge and skills is a direct effect of classroom teaching.

Why can the school's raising students learning effort strategy influence students' further learning development for long term benefit? The reason is that any schools' raising students learning effort strategies can concentrate as much on development as on specific educational outcomes, such as subject knowledge or skill. The review limited to research on " main stream" pupils because inclusion of those will special needs , e.g. the school's poor learning effort students, they feel difficult to raise learning effort or intelligence to achieve pass grade or higher grade (score) in the school.

Thus, it is raising school social responsibility to improve students' learning effort mind. The expectations and treatment of " ready to improve learning effort " to students and schools will feel they have responsibilities to improve studetn learning attitude towards school and better school learning behavior called " school commitment". Thus, it raises schools' interesting to consider how to develop students' long term learning or studying ability in every student individual learning stage.

Hence, any one of raising student's learning effort strategy or method will help schools to feel they have educational responsibilities to help students to learn how to develop their learning effort in their learning career stage. It is beneficial to whole global education development.

The final benefit of raising students learning effort strategies (methods) or skills to any schools implementation, it can achieve three education ideologies development benefits, they include that a conception of changing student individual unlike learning lazy nature, raising their learning interests and assisting their further career development needs. I shall explain every education ideologies development beneficial repect as below:

On raising students learning effort strategies to change student individual unlike learning lazy nature or attiture aspect, the wisest teachers are growing up , should know that general students are lazy to learn. They never consider that students are capable of learning. Students are lazy to learn, it is possible due to they feel some subjects are difficult to learn. For example, it is not mathematics or language in any formal sense that students are taught in the school, in one classroom, some students will be possible feel difficult to learn these subjects. So, it explains why one class will have some students need to be trained from teacher and the teachers need to know how to use different kinds of suitable or useful teaching methods to teach them in order to let the students feel the subject(s) is (are) not difficult to learn as well as to avoid lazy learning factor causes their examination result to be bad. So, such as above mathematics and/or language subjects case, the teacher needs to spend time to use the useful or suitable teaching method to develop mathematics and linguistic skill to let the low effort learning students feel easy to learn these subjects more easy to avoid to cause lazy learning attitude or habit to be caused to them by an artful and well informed teacher, through the educational exploitation of the difficult learning situation of every day.

I shall suggest the solving students lazy learning habit or attitude method, such as " communitiarianisum in education". It includes the conviction that a single, unified community cn be formed from the collection of teachers and pupils that comprise the school; that this community can be and should be more or less isolated from that are taken to be the harmful efforts of modern educational society ; that the student's learning life and the teacher's teaching life of the community are capable of being articulated through norms and rules , which over time can become the student self-lazy learning habit or attitude to a considerable extent, tacit, but which always remain open to modification through conscious action to avoid the student's lazy learning habit cause, due to learning difficult subject(s) reason. The student feels difficult to learn causing factor includes academic, social and emotional element, hence the "curriculum" of the commitarian institution is much broader and much more complex than the activities of the classrooms or the subject(s) listed in the timetable.

Why " commitarian school" can solve the student lazy learing habit or attitude or behavior causes? The reason is that the major tasks of the "commitiarian school" are to create the sub-culture it has itself created to induct outcomes, foster the values it professes and to build up a secure base from which is students can feel difficult learning challenge and confront the wider society.

So " communitiarian school" can bring these benefits to the school. They include: the claim that education, properly organized, can be one of th major forces for planned change in society, the claim that educational processes should be clearly distinguished from certain other social processes, such as commercial advertising, or mass entertainment to raise students learning interests, the aspiration to make a new kind of educator, a conception of learning an acquisition of knowledge as active, social processes involving sobjects, problem solving strategies guides , but not dominated by teachers and the elevation of teachers and other members of a carefully selected and highly trained of educators who are designed the agents of cultural renewal.

Hence, if the school can attempt to achieve communitiarian strategy to communicate with the feeling learning difficult students' parents to enquire their ideas how to persuade their sons or daughters to avoid to make lazy learning habits. Then, it is possible that their sons or daughters will avoid to make lazy habit or behavior to learn when they feel difficult to learn some subjects. So, the effective communication strategy between teachers and students and parents, which will be possible to aovid students make lazy learning habit or behavior when they feel some subjects are difficult to learn.

Anothe raising of student learning effort strategy considers to raise student studying or learning interest beneficial aim. The raising of the student learning effort strategy aim is fundamentally, has been to produce a moral, rational being capable of self-direction and self-responsibility. So, when the student feels he / she has responsibility to learn, then, he /she will have be possible to raise whose learning interest when he / she learns any subjects. Hence, raising of students learning effort strategy will let him / her to feel responsibility to lern and his /her learning / studying interest will be raised in possible when he / she needs to often to read books in classroom or home, due to he /she feels that he/she has responsibility to go to school to learn any subjects.

Hence, learning psychologicl responsibility development of the pupil as it ought to be it makes that pupils feel learning responsibility demands, that is to say, that the pupil can only imperfectly accommodate. It trains contracy to the student individual learning / studying interest and learning expectations of the teacher's raising students learning efforts strtegy at best is supported there is as an element whose function, it is to pursue future economic benefits in terms of better jobs and better salaries intention. Hence, raising students learning effort strategy can let every student to feel that he/she has interest to learn, due to " discipline", " learning responsibility" future better jobs and better salary economic reward and poor jobs and poor salary punishment effort to cause he /she will feel examination grades to be low , due to he/she discovers to lack interest to learn any subjects reason. For example, physical , education , various arts and crafts, a variety of practice skills, domestic science and the like emphasise doing much learning responsibility of subjects, rather than pure cognition, though there is usually an intellectual learning element. For another example, English , a modern language, history, geography, social science, technical mathematics etc. subjects , they are the disciplines that play a major role of learning responsibility to every student. So, these subjects will be easily to train students to rause learning / studying responsibility in order to raise their learning / studying interests more easily.

It will bring one interesting question. Will school learners find the opportunities to pursue any interest , they may have found in practising modern educational dance, pottery, drama, even art and music subjects? The mass media comprise the real cultural life (apart from hobbies) to conventional subjects in the cultural life of the school. Hence, it seems that learning responsibility can be arised from the student's interest to learn the subjects , e.g. if the student has interest to learn music, dance , art etc. non-conventional subjects. Then, his /her interest will raise his/her responsibility feeling to learn any one of these non-conventional subjects because the hobbies influence their learning behavior to learn these subjects. However, I recommend any schools need to students to feel they have learning responsibilities to learn the conventional subjects, e.g. language , mathematics, economy, geography, science, psychology, education, history , biology, engineering, earth science, media etc. subjects. So, when the students feel that they have learning responsibilities to learn any one of these subjects, then they will be trained to feel interests to learn these subjects or study any one of these subjects. It is one effective learning method to raise students' learning effort. Hence, the raising of students learning strategy , it can be beneficial to raise conventional subjects of learning students learning responsibility and learning interests in order to achieve to let them to exam the better grade (score) more easily.

In the latter benefit of assistance students further carrer development needs aspect, I believe the raising of students learning effort strategy can bring this kind of benefit to assist studnts to learn or know how to develop their further career in the corrective learning way or attitude. After the school's students feel that they can earn better examination grades(scrores), due to their school has achieved to raise their learning effort successfully. They will feel disciplines and efficient learning needs that is very important to influence their further career development as well as they will also feel learning by means of disciplines is made easier or more efficient, when they feel that they have learning responsibility to learn any subjects.

Hence, raising of students learning effort which will influence students to believe or feel education should be based not only on knowledge , but on the separate disciplines, such as learning responsibility or term of knowledge , such as whose interests to choose to learn the subjects is accepted.

Consideration to how raising of students learning effort strategies or methods or skills which can assist students further career development. It based on these ideas. The most immediate response necessary is a changed relationship between work and school, but work experience programmes are still barely integrated into the ongoing processes of the school and school's career advice services are still considered to studrnt individual skills, talents and presences with present job opportunities. In this process, finding and holding a job are the limits of career advice . Thus, if the school's students feel their schools' teachers have good teaching methods or teaching skills or teaching strategies to help them to raise their learning effort effectively. Then, the school will let students to feel it is considering their further career development, even when they have graduated and leave this school to further study plan to find job. Thus, this schhol will let students feel that it is not only teach themm to learn new knowledge aim, it also considers their further career development. Thus, its number of students will have possible to increase, due to students feel it considerates their further career development, such as an objective for working, class schools and their curriculim would be to show that work is planned, organized , negotiated and distributed, that one is part of a pattern of employment and that not all consideration of work relate to personal talent, desire or liking. In sum, the forces that shape employment and work can be examined and understood. Hence, the purpose of working -class schools would not only be to study or learn these phenomena and actually experience some work.

How can raise student learning effort to encourage they consider their further career development? I want to take seriously the concepts of work, class and learning in goinf vs these points of orientation in beginning the difficult and complex tasks of thinking about a working-class school to students. But, these concepts don't just serve as points of orientation, I want to argue that a relation to work and learning to one student's class positive and to domination over others is taught in our schools. These are schools in our education system which do actually perform a must active, and quite conscious function in terms of training their pupils for work, equipping them with the right learning attitudes or habits and beliefs to hole their place in society and to acquire the resources to enforce compliance and respect their further career development when the school can let its students feel its aim to raise their learning effort in order to educate them enough knowledge to assist them to develop their carer in any jobs aspect.

These schools teach their pupils about work,class and teach it about any knowledge extremely well relates to job. They are precisely the schools (both private and public) that are long and successful academic and social tradition. They teach their students' parents ,such as their sons and daughters of the well-to-do and the ambitions the tools of raising of students job effort knowledge: How to manipulate and control social job-relatived knowledge to let them to think it is a real job knowledge learning school to attribute further career development benefit to prepare their further career development.

Consequently, raising of students learning efforts strategy can let studetns to think the school is a real job knowledge learning school to attract many students to choose to study to win its education competitors in education industry more easily.

How to create effective teaching and learning environments?

An good and effective teaching method and learning environment can assist students to raise learning efforts indirectly. I shall focus on lower secondary education in both the public and private sectors, how to create effective teaching and learning environments to raise teachers' teaching abilities, training teachers' corrective beliefs or teaching attitudes, and teaching positive practices and raising school leadership efforts in schools.

What are the factors to influence teachers and school principals to raise teaching efforts and school leadership efforts of effective and good education system in any schools and classrooms? Whether has it close relationship between effective education systems and raising students' learning efforts?

It looks at a range of featcures that shape teaching and learning, which has closing relationship to raise students efforts. But how strongly do these characteristics affect learning itself? However, it looks at important features that shape effective learning. Special emphasis was given: TO how successful teachers feel in addressing the educatinal challenges who face (self-efficacy) and to what extent classrooms are orderly and conductive to learning classroom disciplinary climate.

Some past education researchs indicate classroom climate not only has been shown to affect student outcomes and attainment , but is a prominent policy issue in a number of countries and regions. The actions of students within classrooms and the creation of a safe and produce learning environment are important for many schools and can be a influential challenges of teachers' work.

On the one hand, however, these past education researchs concluded at how factors, such as aspects of teacher individual professional development or varying teaching methods were associated with self-efficacy and classroom disciplinary climate. It sums up then adjusted this effect for background factors, such as socio-economic characteristics of schools consequently for each factor, for which significant effects has been found , additional estimates accounted for factors in other categories where the effects were significant.

On another hand, the educational researchs also indicated that between factors, such as a positive school climate, teaching beliefs, co-operation betwen teachers, teacher job satisfaction, professional development and th adoption of different teaching techniques. The factors , much of the variation identified was in differences among individual teachers rather then among schools.

The implication is that by addressing teachers' attitudes, beliefs and teaching practices experiences are as a whole. This is scope for considerable improvement in teaching and learning, but that this way require individualized support for teachers rather than just whole- school or whole-organizational students , whole school-educational system. On the other hand, the educational researchs also indicated the appraisal and feedback, which teachers receive is mirrored in the beliefes, in their own teaching abilities, in other words, when they receive feedback on their teaching work, the more they turst in their abilities to address teaching challenges. So, encouraging teacher or their teaching abilities appraisal to some excellent teaching performance teachers, it can create effective teaching and learning environments indirectly, due to these good teaching performance teachers have good emotion to teach in classrooms by schools appraisal.

In fact, student individual satisfaction, it has cause and affect relationship between or unsatisfactied to whose teacher's teaching demand and good or bad teaching and learning environment. It means that when many students will feel more satisfied to whose teachers' teaching demand, it is general due to the school's teachers can raise good teaching and learning environments to their students. Hence, if the school teachers expect to raise their teaching performances. I suggest that they need to participate in qualification courses commit considerable time and money to these courses, when which their thinking are effective. Yet relatively few participation in this type of activity and those who do often feel frustrated by the lack of sufficient time to devote to them. This suggests time and money made available to teacher for such courses.

Consequently, good and effective teaching and learning

environments can help students to raise whose learning efforts, due to they will have good learning emotion to learn in classrooms. It is one kind of positive teaching and learning psychological method to be used to raise students learning efforts.

● Raising knowledge and skills in educator method

Future educators need to be raised knowledge and skills in their major subject aspect, they need to prepare to programs of research and evaluation of 21 ST century education, educator preparation programs will be recognized as sources of leadership in developing 21ST century education and learning strategies. Each educator preparation program will develop a 21 ST century blueprint for transforming itself into a 21 ST century program, higher education leaders will work with leaders in local communities to inform the redesign of education preparation programs to more effectively meet the needs of 21 ST century learners, new teachers will be prepared to become change knowledge and skills in all subjects in accordance with national standards. If they expect to raise students' learning effort in short term successfully. Future teachers are asked to achieve significant academic growth to all students at the same time, but they instruct students with even more diverse needs. Teaching has never been more difficult, it has never been more important, and the desperate need for more student success has been raised need.

On the one hand, I shall indicate many successful engage in strategies to assist teachers to raise teaching knowledge level, such as : Providing high quality alternative routes to teaching , building on private and public partnerships that share common sets of ideas in advancing education reforms, e.g. effectively partnering with urban schools to prepare teacher canadidates to teach in urban environments with large numbers of urban school learners' raising learning effort needs, playing a greater role with charter and other experimental / alternative schools, effectively recruiting career changes to build the teacher workforce , creating a robust clinical experience for teacher candidates, including year long teaching of learning how to raise students' learning effort programs, growing a network of over 1,000 raising students' learning effort research development schools to attempt to helpt to find any methods which can raise students' learning effort effectively.

On the other hand, in order to meet the challenges and demands of the poor learning effort of students. I suggest that as below: schools ought provide evidence that the teachers prepared at the raising students' learning effort and member institutions will have a positive effect on their students' learning, going beyond providing content knowledge and prepare teachers to differentiate their institution to reach all poor learning effort students especially.

The most at risk for school failure: Low income homes' students, poor english language learners, poor learning effort of students with disabilities, ensuring that teacher candidates receive extensive , in-depth how to raise students' learning effort experiences with mentoring support that requires teaching to poor learning effor of students' performance evaluation tied to the teacher licensure process and high standards for beginning practice, creating fast, track, yet high teaching quality , raising students; learning effort of teacher preparation programs in close partnership with school districts to meet specific teacher shortages in order to train future many teachers who have efforts to assist to raise student's learning effort to pursue top-performing student number to be raised successfully.

On the one hand, how to raise teacher's teaching effort in order to raise student learning ability? The important themes will include: Global awareness, e.g. understanding global issues, other nations and other culture, financial , economic, business and entrepreneurial literacy, e.g. knowing how to make economic choices, understanding the role of the economy in society, civic literacy, e.g. learning how to participate effectively in civic life, exercising the rights and obligations of citizenship, high literacy, e.g. obtaining interpreting and understanding basic methods how to raise student' learning effort in short term. On the other hand, future teachers also need have learning and innovation skills, e.g. critical thinking and problem solving, effectively analyze and evaluate evidence, argument, cliams and beliefs, solve different kinds of non-familiar problems in both conventional and innovative ways: Effective communication skill, e.g. articulate thoughts and ideas effectively using oral and writtn communication skills iin a variety of forms and contexts; effective collaboration skill, e.g. demonstrate ability to work effective and respectfully with diverse teams; creativity and innovation ability , e.g. use a wide range of idea creation techniques to create new and worthwhile ideas. They also need to learn information, media and technology skills, e.g. access and evaluate information critically and competently; manage the flow of information from a wide variety of sources; understanding both how and why media messages are constructed; creating media products by understanding and utilizing the most appropriate media creation tools; characteristics and conventions; learning how to use technology as a tool to research ; organize and evaluate and communicate information.

Finally, they need to know life and career skills, e.g. flexibility and adaptability, initiative and self-direction, social and cross cultural skills productivity and accountability, leadership and responsibility. Consequently, when future teachers can be trained to own these skills. Then, they will have ability to prepare how to raise students' learning efforts in future global education industry development more easily.

Teaching to use data in school improvement efforts

What are teaching to use data in school improvement efforts? Why and how can teaching to use data in school improve students' learnings efforts? How to integrate data to raise school improvement process? Why has the need for data instead of intuition, tradition and convenience to guide administrative and educational decisions become increasingly important?

I shall indicate why educators need to learn how to use data in their schools to improve planning process in order to raise students' learning efforts more easily. I shall also indicate some foundational information on types of data, strategies for analyzing and understanding data and methods for determining how these efforts can influence goals and planning.

The types of data that educators can use to define their problems and needs, select improvement strategies and goals, change and monitor progress. These data includes achievement data, demographic data, program data and perception data. They will be useful to be applied to raise students' learning efforts by teachers (educators). For this situation example, a school leader needs to meeting to discuss how to solve one problem solving issue, pooling their knowledge, talent and ideas. The leader and his/her other school department leaders need to join teachers, support and parents in teams to explore students' learning improvement issues. How to say that gathering data to prepare to discuss this issue which can raise their leadership skills in creating numerous and diverse partnerships, sustaining a vision, focusing on group problem-solving, using conflicts resolution in order to conclude the most useful ideas or methods to raise the school's students learning efforts. Because every school's environment situation, learning environment, school and teachers' qualities , teaching experiences, students' learning efforts, kinds of courses are different. So, they need time to gather data to prepare every different meeting discussion topics to already discuss any challenges about teaching, the time will be long or short to gather data to prepare every meeting discussion to cause time preparation challenge. For example, the process enquires time, time during the day and the week , even on month or more to involve teachers always cause a time meeting preparation and meeting discussion time challenge. If the meeting discussion topic is experienced and difficult to gather data , then it will need to arrange longer time to prepare the meeting and the meeting time. Otherwise, if the meeting discussion topic is not experienced and simple to gather data, then will need to arrange shorter time to prepare the meeting and the meeting time. If one week , the school only has one meeting , then it is not a time arrangement problem to prepare the meeting. But, supposing the schools has ten departments and if one week the school's every department has at least one meeting , even more than one meeting to prepare time to discuss different kinds of teaching challenges and the school's resource and rooms are not enough, So, the school must need have good time arrangement to be organized to gather data and pre-booking rooms for the ten meetings at least or more. Hence, every school is committed to use data to guide its work allocate time for teachers to meet, discuss, reflect upon data and make informed instructional decisions. Schools identify the need for this time, then find it through a combination of creative scheduling (e.g. having all good grader teachers share student data , when students attend a interesting course, e.g. art and music , sport and priority setting, e.g. using one to three maximum weekly faculty meetings to analyze student data). Thus, data can help to build a district and school culture that values the use of reliable, complete information to guide their every meeting decisions and solve problems more effectively. Although, for many school meeting members, they will have idea to feel difficult of working with data is unfamiliar and perhaps uncomfortable. But the fact is, whether teachers need to realize data or not, they use data every data to help make any decisions, data will help them to make decisions about school improvement more accurately.

How to apply data gathering method to improve every student learning effort challenge? If schools are to provide learning environments that are meaningful and engaging, educators must continually reflect on the quality of school systems and focus their efforts to make them better.

Firstly, the school needs have an effective learning improvement cycle. The school improvement cycle includes four major activities: plan (developing a plan for improvement) implement the plan, (study) ,evaluate the impact according to specific criteria action (adjust strategies to better meet criteria).

How to apply data gathering for this school improvement plan? Data are the key to continuous improvement. When the school plans, it must for its goals. Data patterns reveal strengths and weaknesses in the school plan system and provide excellent direction. When the school does (acts) the school collect, data that will tell the teachers what the impact of their strategies are between the school and teachers. Through collaborative reflection, the school leaders " studies" the feedback offered by its teachers data and begins to understand when to stay the course and then to make changes. Then, the school can act to refine what are the best raising students learning efforts strategies.

Eventually, the whole cycle begins again. The data throughout the school improvement cycle can be applied to help teachers to gather to make decision making regarding student learning as below:

The data gathering driven decision making based on intuition, tradition or convenience includes focused staff development programs, as an improvement strategy to solve documented problems needs, budget allocations to programs based on data-informed need, staff assignments based on skills needed as indicated by the data, organized factual reports to the community about the learning progress of students, goal-setting based on data about problems and possible explanations, staff meeting that focus on strategies and issues raised by the local school's data, regular parent communication record regarding the progress of their children learning effort record, grading systems based on common student performance criteria that report progress on the standards as well as work skills and past administrative team meeting that focus on measured progress toward data-based improvement goals.

Hence, an effective and efficient data in school improvement efforts record system can help teachers to gather data regarding every different challenge to let them to uses actual data to further discuss data analysis to assist school leaders in the creation of research-based strategies data –based goals and make an evaluation plan to measure results in order to achieve the most effective methods to solve students learning effort raising challenge.

Consequently, I recommend that every school needs to understand what it is building knowledge around different aspects of school improvement processes, it can get started learning about how to use data in above those areas in order to achieve how to implement the most effective methods to solve students learning efforts raising challenge. For example, they include that how to record data to develop a leadership team, how to collect various types of data , how to analyze data patterns, how to generate hypotheses, how to develop goal-setting guideline, how to design specific raising students' learning effort strategies, how to define evaluation criteria and how to make the commitment to let students who feel that their learning efforts are raised by their teachers. Hence, efficient and systematic data gathering record system tool can assist any schools to give opinions to make decisions to achieve strategies to raise students' learning effort more accurate, due to past all data is the school's actual record, it can reflect all past every student learning performance in order to let teachers to make more accurate judgement to decide whether to choose the method(S) is (are) the most suitable and effective solution(S) to raise student learning effort.

Teaching and classroom learning method

School leaders and teachers both have responsibilities to attempt to find what methods can raise student learning effort in their schools in education industry. Which aspects of consideration are needed to think about what they wish to assess. I shall access as below:

On teachers' consideration aspect, the qualities of teachers who wish to access include: How to organize subject matter and courses, how to communicate between students and students' parents, how much knowledge of the subject matter, who is familiar to teach, how much enthusiasm for the subject and for teaching, how the teacher's attitude toward students, how fairness in testing and grading, how flexibility in approaches to teaching, how appropriateness of student learning outcomes. All of above factors will influence every students' learning efforts in the school.

So, every teacher needs to find or choose which aspects can influence his/her teaching qualities to be poor and how he/she wishes to assess it in order to improve / raise his/her teaching performance to satisfy students' learning needs.

They can collect data in many ways in order to assess which aspects of teaching methods need to be improved. They ways include: structured interviews with students, instructional rating surveys, tests and exams, content analysis of instructional materials and review of classroom records.

When, he/she had chosen methods to assess the effectiveness of his/her teaching. He/she needs to follow these guidelines: avoiding technologies that don't appeal to his/her intuition and judgement as a teacher, not allowing and self- assessment to become a burden, choosing techniques that will benefit m/herself and his/her students, planning how to introduce the techniques to students, estimating and planning for how much class time it will take, not using these techniques for often, if the students find them predictable, the information won't be as useful , needing brief written exercises are good for encouraging shy students to express their thoughts, encouraging students to be frank without the possibility of penalty, remembering that assessment and analysis probably take twice as long as he/she thinks and allowing enough time to plan for teaching method change.

What will students be influenced from the teacher's teaching method change after he/she assessed which aspects are needed to influence his/her teaching performance to be poor? Usually, qualities students want in an instructor to willingness to take extra time to answer questions and solve problems, well organized presentations and lessons , real world experts respect for students and sense. All of these requirements are students whose expectation to every teacher's teaching attitude and quality or performance.

Teachers have responsibilities to do these behaviors in classroom. They include: students attendance record, student participation in classroom activities and her/his own feelings record three aspects. For example, one student attendance record aspect, the class of student attendance records. Do students miss a particular class or activity? It aims to find what the seasons to influence the student often absent, e.g. he/she has less interest in this topic of activity and this attitude is being communicated to the student or perhaps the student doesn't understand why certain content is important or may be the way the teacher delivers his/her lectures needs to be more lively or interactive or personal issues cause absent, e.g. medical problems, religious and cultural activities can affect student attendance and learning performance.

On student participation in classroom activities aspect, teachers need to know whether students are more involved at certain times than at others. Do they often or sometimes ask questions? Why do they not like to ask questions? Do they request extra resource material? What is their need? Hence, teachers ought be often observant note their reactions to something they do or say. If students, are not sure the teachers perception is right, try something similar again and see if the student reaction repeats.

On teachers' own feeling aspect, every teacher needs to know themselves feeling. Does the teacher aware of whose own feeling as he/she teaches? His /her feeling may be sad, angry, enjoyable, excited, depressed, worried. When the teacher recognize his/her feeling, he/she can examine the actions (his/her own and the students) that led to these feeling. Their mood and feeling will affect whose students, and their mood will also affect the teacher's teaching actions. Hence, teacher's mood will influence every class student's learning effort in the classroom, if the teacher has enjoyable mood to teach his /her students, then his her teaching mood and behavior will influence his /her efforts to raise more nervous to teach whose students to learn in the classroom.

Another discussion issue concerns how to access classroom learning. Classroom assessment will make a strong contribution to the improvement of learning . In classroom, how students; feedback to the teacher's teaching contents. It is one important factor to raise student's effort to learn because feedback is more reflective theoretical, presenting, grounded in evidence of the nature of feedback , a concept , which is central to formative assessment. Hence, when the teacher may receive either positive or negative feedback form his/her students immediately in the classroom. Then, his / her can know whether his/her teaching what weaknesses are for her/her teaching method or skill. Then, he/she can concentrate on revise the weaknesses to avoid next occurrence to let students to feel her /his teaching performance is poor or unsatisfactory due to whose teaching weaknesses cause as well as he /she can know how to revise whose teaching weaknesses and improve whose teaching skill or method more clearly.

Another considerable aspect is that learning or teaching system aspect , schools need to consider that the grading function is whether over-emphasized and/or the learning function under-emphasized. There is a tendency to use a normative rather than a criterion approach, which emphasizes competition between pupils rather than personal improvement of each.

The evidence is that with such practices the effect of feedback is to teach the whether pupils that they lack ability. So, that they are de-motivated and lose confidence in their own capability to learn strategies for " slow learners" to raise learning. In general, it is difficult to discover (find) who are the slow learners, slow learners in the regular classroom are neither rare nor unique. Slow learner is one who can't learn at an average rate form the instructional resources, text, workbooks, and learning materials that are designed for the majority of students in the classroom. These students need special instructional frequent feedback, corrective institution and/or modified materials, all administered under conditions sufficiently flexible for learning to occur.

I shall recommend that slow leaders are usually taught in one of two possible instructional arrangements: The first is that a class composed mostly of average students , in which case up to 20% may be slow learners or the second is that a class specially designed for slow learner. The most obvious characteristics is a limited attention to compare to more able students.

However, I believe these teaching methods can be used to attempt to raise slow learners' attention during they need to listen teachers' speaking in any class time. The first kind is compensatory teaching method, it is an instructional approach that alters the presentation of content to a student's fundamental weakness or deficiency. This teaching method recognizes contents, transmits through alternate modalities (pictures versus words, and supplements it with additional learning resources and activities) learning centers and group discussion, and co-operative learning. It aims to give pictures, films, visual representation of contents what the teacher's teaching speaking is. Another kind is remedial teaching. This is an alternate approach for the regular classroom teacher in instructing the slow learner . It is the use of activities, techniques and practices to eliminate weaknesses or deficiency that the slow learner is known to have. For example, deficiencies in basic math calculation skills learning effort are reduced or eliminated by re-teaching the content that was not learned earlier. The instructional environment does not change, as in the compensatory approach. Conventional instructional techniques such as practice might be used.

In conclusion, every teacher needs to learn which kind of teaching and classroom learning method or technique is the most suitable skill in order to raise whose students' learning effort to learn easily. So, learning which kind of teaching method is important to influence the teacher's performance to be improved to influence each student's learning mood in classroom ad he/she needs to spend time to find which are whose teaching challenges to need to be improved.

Educational training tools for raising student learning effort development

Improving students' learning with effective learning techniques, knowing which kinds of educational training tools which can raise students' learning effort that is very important. Because every school has different educational method(s), so , it causes every school ought choose the most suitable kind(s) of educational training tool(S) to raise its students learning effort. I shall indicate some kinds of educational training tools to raise students learning effort as below:

Firstly, it is direction from cognitive educational psychological method. The techniques include elaborative interrogation, self exploration, summarization, highlighting, the keyword mnemonic, imagery use for text learning, re-reading , practice testing , distributed practice and interleaved practice.

When every student learns, who needs to read the book , how to raise his/her reading effort to know all main contents (main points) of any books' chapter(s). What mean of the chapter is? It is very important to let the student really remembers or knows the chapter contents or what the author's writing mean of the books' chapter/ So, in educational psychological view point, summarization , highlighting, the key word mnemonic , imagery use for text , learning and re-reading technique can help every student to rise effort to remember the chapter's contents. For example, summarization and imagery use for text learning have been shown to help some students on some criterion tasks, but yet the conditions under which these techniques produce benefits are limited, and much research is still needed to fully explore their overall effectiveness.

The keyword mnemonic is difficult to implement in some contexts, and it appears to benefit students for a limited number of materials and for short retention intervals. However, more students report re-reading and highlighting, yet these techniques do not consistently boost students' performance. So many students like to use practice testing instead of re-reading techniques when they are reading any books.

About above those reading techniques, I bring some questions: If simple techniques were available that teachers and students could use to improve student learning and achievement, whether every student's learning performance will be poor if the teacher was not being told about those techniques and if many students were not using them? What if students were instead adopting ineffective learning techniques that undermined their achievement or at least did not improve their prior ineffective learning techniques?

To assess above questions. We need to know whether what different learning benefits to the student. I shall explain every kinds of learning technique benefits to students as below:

Flaborative interrogation means generating an explanation for why a stated fact or concept is true. Self explanation means explaining how new information is related to known information is related to known information , or explaining steps taken during problem solving, summaries means writing , summaries of various lengths of to be learned texts, highlighting means making potentially important portions of to be learned materials when reading, keyword mnemonic means using keywords and mental imagery to associate verbal materials, imagery for text means attempting to form mental images of text materials when reading or listening, re-reading means restudying text material again after an initial reading, practice testing means self-testing or taking practice tests over –to-be-learned, distributed practice means implementing a schedule of practice that spreads out study activities over time, interleaved practice means implementing a schedule of practice that mixes different kinds of material within a single study session. So, every kind of learning technique will have different reading or learning benefits to adapt to every student's different reading habit or personal reading need. If the student expected to raise whose learning effort in short time. He/she must need to know whether which kind of learning technique(s) can be the most useful or suitable to him/her to use in whose learning or reading practice.

I shall indicate what the suitable learning materials and learning condition are for the different kind of student characteristics to be adapted in order to raise whose learning effort need as below:

Materials remember words cards is suitable to be used in amount of reading remember practices learning condition and age is student characteristics , material translation equivalents is suitable to be used in open vs closed book practice learning condition and prior domain knowledge is student characteristics, lecture content materials is suitable to be used in reading vs listening learning condition and working memory capacity is student characteristics, science definition materials is suitable to be used in incidental vs intentional learning condition and verbal ability is student characteristics, narrative texts can be used on direct instruction learning condition and interests is student characteristics, expository texts can be used on discovery learning condition and intelligence is studied characteristics, mathematical concepts can be used on rereading lags learning condition and motivation is students characteristics, maps can be used on kind of prior achievement is student characteristics , diagrams can be used on group vs individual learning condition and self efficacy is student characteristics.

Hence, every school needs to know very student's learning characteristics and what the learning techniques in order to achieve to raise every individual student's learning effort effectively.

Instead of learning techniques can be attempted to use to raise training activities and teachers' teaching abilities, it will also be one important factor to raise students' learning efforts. There are five key areas of student assessment as below:

Firstly, the school needs to know how inclusive education is the school current student assessment system. This activity takes readers through a series of tasks linking student assessment to the inclusive education. Secondly, the school needs to know how to make student assessment contribute to better quality and more inclusive education. The school will need introduce interesting practices and models that promote greater inclusivity in education, including the development of formative assessment, the use of summative assessment, for inclusive progress and the design and use of quality educational methods for student assessment. Thirdly, the school needs to know what basic competencies are needed to make student assessment more inclusive. The basic competencies (knowledge, skills , values , attitudes, etc.) that are required to access the student learning in inclusive education. Fourthly, the school needs to know what the relationship between student assessment at different levels, such as intentional, regional, national and school levels, as well as various countries' approaches to these assessments. Finally, the school needs to know how to adopt an approach to student assessment. It needs to introduce a series of tools and models for student assessment education system and society . Thus, the purpose of training activities to the school that lets the school teachers who can analyze or apply assessment practices in response to specific student learning challenges or issues that the schools' teachers may encounter during the educational process. The school teachers may be required to do this individual as a raising student learning effort topic meeting of the school. Consequently, student educational techniques and teaching improvement effort activities techniques will be one good method to raise student learning effort method.

Reference

Buyees, V., Sparkman, K. L. & Wesley, P. W. (2003). communities of practice; connecting what we know with what we do, exceptional children, 69(3), 263-277.

Cook-Sather, A. (2002). Authorizing students; perspectives: Toward trust, Dialogue and change in education, education researcher, 31(4), 3-14.

Cook-Sather, A. (2009) from traditional accountability to shared responsibility: The benefits and challenges of student consultants gathering midcourse feedback in college classrooms assessment evaluation in higher education 34(2), 231-241.

Fielding, M. (2006) leadership radical student engagement and the necessity of person- centered education. International Journal of leadership in education , 9 (4) , 299-313.

Good, T. F. & Brophy, J, (1986). School effects. In M. Wittrock 9 ed.) handbook of research on teaching (pp. 570-602). New York : Macmillan.

Lewis, K.G. (2001). Using midsemester student feedback and responding to it. New directions for teaching and learning 87(3) 33.44.

Seale, J. (2010). Doing student voice work in higher education: An exploration of the value of participatory methods. British educational research journal, 36(6) , 995-1015.

Warren , M. (2005), communities and schools: A new view of urban school reform. Harvard educational review, 75(2), 133-173.

Raising learning interest

Behavioral economic solves classroom management discipline

How to apply behavioral economic method to help teachers to solve classroom management discipline in order to raise student indiviudal learning interest in classrooms? Students need to know what classroom management means. It means effective discipline, it is being prepared to motivate students to raise interesting to learn in classrooms. It is providing a safe, comfortable learning environment, it can build the teacher individual student's sale esteem and creative and imaginative in daily lessons.

Why has classroom management relationship to student individual behavior as well as why behavioral economic method can be applied to solve classroom management discipline in possible? It is simple because every teacher teaching styles, personality attitudes and every teacher managment strategies are different and are not effective. It is possible that due to teaching experiences. Student population to every lesson, low or high salary level, every teacher individual time preparation and time management factors. Then all issues concern whether every teacher to do choice to arrange whose time to prepare before he/she will teach which lesson on that day. For example, if the teacher feels tried to teach more than fine lessons on that day, because he/she is sick. But the school has no enough teachers number to replace the student to teach his/her students on that day. So, he/her teaching performance can not b better , satisfaction and enjoyment in teaching are dependent upon how he/she leads students to cooperate.

Hence, he/she can not permit to so personal rest behavioral choice, and he/she feels that salary can not be raised to double payment or more to get overtime allowance on that teaching day. It will bring any unsatisfactory and unenjoyable teaching attitude or poor teaching behavior or performance and teacher won't deal with discruptive behaviors. Buy, also manage to minimize off task, non-disruptive teaching behavior to teach students and manage their own behavior to learn in classroom effectively and efficiently. Their poor classroom management behavior will bring poor teaching performance. Hence, students won't feel the school teachers are good teachers and students' families will lose confidence to let the school teachers to teach their students.

In Behavioral economic teaching method view point, the school needs to review whether its teachers number is enough to prepare some teachers need to rest at home suddenly. So, other teachers can replace them to teach any his/her lessons on that day immediately. If the school neglected to employ extra enough part time teachers number to prepare to replace any full time teachers who have need to rest on any days. Due to salary expenditure increasing reason, it is not good choice to reduce to employ extra part time teachers number to avoid the sudden full time teachers numbe shortage need. It will bring classroom management changes poor, due to unsatisfactory teachers' teaching need to go to classroom to teach their students in classrooms when they are sicknessess on that teaching day suddenly. Therefore, poor teaching performance or poor classroom management behaviors to the teacher which will bring poor economic loss, e.g. student enrollment number reduces, students absent number to every lesson increases school teaching subjects number decreases too the school in long time.

Therefore, all these poor influences will cause the school's economic loss, it is due to the school teachers' teaching behaviors are poor , due to many teachers do not enjoy and feel satisfactory to teach these students and manage classes disciplines effectively. It seems that whether the school has enough teachers number, it can infuence how teacher individual teaching and class management behavior to be better or worse and then which will have relationship to influence the school's economic gain or loss in long term consequently.

Therefore, in teacher individual behavioral psychological view point, every one ought have effective time allocation method to prepare how to teach whose students in every lesson. I shall recommend how the teacher individual behavioral economic choice to solve discipline challenges in classrooms as below:

1. Transitions vs. allocated time method

The school teachers can allocate time periods they intend for their students to be engaged in learning activities as well as they can arrange transition time allocated for learning activities. For example, getting students assembled and attentive, assigning reading and directing to begin, getting students' attention away from reading and preparing for class discussion in their schools.

The transition is allocated time to teacher individual behavioral goal is to increase the variety of learning activities , but to decrease transition time, student engagement and non-task behaviors are dependent on how smoothly and efficiently to teachers more from one learning activity to another.

Therefore, teacher has withitness if when classroom discipline problems occue, the teache consistently takes action to solve the misbehavior of exactly those students who do in classrooms, when two discipline problems arise as the same time, the teacher can deal with the more serious first. The teacher can decisively handle instances of off- task behavior before the behaviors either set out of hand or are modeled by others. When handling misbehavior makes sure all students learn what is unacceptable about that behavior, deal with misbehavior without disrupting the learning activity.

2. Classroom rules for student individual behavioral conduct. Formalized statements that provide students with general guidelines for the types of behaviors that are require and the types that are prohibited a few rules are easier to remember than many rules, each rule in a small set of rules is more important than each rule in a large set of rules.

Why do need necessary classroom rules of conduct? It aims to maximize on -task behaviors and minimize off-task (esp, discuptive) behaviors, secures the safety and comfort of the learning environment, prevents the activities of the class from disturbing other classes, establish an learning environment in which achieving specified learning goals takes priority over other concerns in classrooms, be particularly prepared and organized to minimize transition time and utilizes a communication style that establishing non-threatening, comfortable environment to let students to learn in classrooms. Other components of disclosure statement include: basis course outline, grading procedures, include procedures for making up missed work, extra credit homework expected etc., attendance policies should be consistent with school policy, other class rules, policies procedures, safety considerations as necessary , accommodation for disabilities statement, signature of student and parent / guardian. Therefore, classroom rules can influence how student individual chooses to do whose learning conduct or behavior , even improving their learning attidude in classrooms. Classroom rules are the best method fo influence every student how to choose to do whose learning behaviors in classroom in order to earn the most effective learning benefits for themselves.

Finally, I shall discuss how to apply behavioral economic mehod to raise student learning interest at classrooms? As I explained that when teacher feels that individual satisfactory or enjoyable teaching feeling to do his/her teaching job,which will influence whose teaching performance in classrooms. Thus, how to improve every teacher individual teaching performance or method or teaching quality which will be important factor to influence whose student individual learning interest to be raised in classrooms indirectly.

I recommend that teachers need to concern how to arrange classroom teaching environment to be attractive or safe or enjoyable to influence every student individual learning attitude to increase more attention or concentate to hear whose teacher's teaching to his/her any lessons in the classroom more considerately. Arrangement is determined by learning activity (lecture, class discussion, small group work etc. learning activities in classrooms). Thinking thorugh class procedure and learning activities and arrangement the classroom in the best possible way.

Teachers need to know why the student chooses to do his/her behavior in classroom. Usually, every behavior has a function , three primary reasons for disputive behavior in the classroom include power, attention, wnat to be left alone (i.e. disinterest or feelings of inadequacy). Many misbehavior are exhibited by students are responses to a behavior needs exhibited by the teacher to understand why a person exhibits behavior is no reason to tolerate it, teacher needs to understand the function of a behavior will help in knowing how to deal with that behavior. When, the teacher can understand why the student chooses to do his/her behavior to find the solutions to persuade or dissuade the student does not choose to do the harmful behavior or change the harmful behavior to do right behavior in order to influence other students can not concentrate on learning considerately.

Consequently, if th school expected to raise every student individual learning interest in classrooms. The school needs to find methods to let its teachers feel satisfactory to teach their students in the school as well as the school's teachers need to learn how to understand why the student chooses to do harmful behavior to influence other students concentrate on easier learning in an enjoyable learning classroom environment.

When the school can let its teachers to enjoy to do their teaching jobs and they can feel more satisfactory when they are teaching every time in classroom as well as its teachers can understand some students why they choose to do harmful learning behavior to influence the other students to concentrate on learning in classrooms and they can find the solvable methods to dissuade they do not choose to do harmful learning behavior ro influence other students can not conentrate on learning in clssrooms again. Then, between the school's teachers and students both can build positive teaching attitudes and learning attitudes in order to cause they can choose to do enjoyable and satisfactory teaching behaviors or performances to teacher and concentration on learning behavior or attitues to students in classrooms.

Consequently, when the school can build a good classroom learning environment to let teachers consider to teach their students in order to bring whose students can concentrate on learning in classrooms. Then, a good classroom learning environment will bring good learning economic and non-economic benefit , such as student number increases , school income increases and teachers salaries increase, student individual attention will raise, student will enjoy to go to school and absence number will reduce. Consequently, any schools' teacher individual teaching behvior and student individual learning behavior both in classrooms which must have positive or negative relationship to bring the school itself and the teachers themselves long term economic and non-economic benefits in learning behavioral economic view point. Also, the importance is that learning behavioral economic analysis, can explain why the teacher individual good or bad emotion can influence his/her every lesson student individual learning emotion to be good or bad to do learning behavior in clasroom. So, schools need to concern every teacher individual emotion whether he/she feels enjoyable or satisfactory to teach his/her students in classrooms in order to avoid every classroom students' learning emotion will be influenced to be poor to bring long time economic loss to the school. It is one importnat factor to influence any school's teaching performance to be succeed.

Successful persuasive teaching method can raise student individual learning behavior
Can teachers apply behavioral economic method to raise student individual learning behavior? Behavioral economic method is explained by psychology and other disciplines to create models of limits on rationality, willpower and self-interest. Although, economic professionals believe it can be applied to predict consumer behavior. But, how any why can it be applied to raise student personal interest to learn new knowledg in education industry aspect? This is one valuable research question. If it can be appled to eduational psychology aspect to raise student individual learning interesting influentially, educators ought need to learn to how to do in order to persuade student indivudal has more interest to learn in anywhere schools or homes or libraries in habitually persuasively. I shall explain some possible educational psychological methods as below:
When one student discovered that learning will bring much tangible and intangible benefits to infulence his/her career development in the future. For example, he/she can find good jobs, earn more salaries, raise the high class social positon, build personal successgul image or raise satisfactory feeling, raise social competitive effort in job market etc. different economic related benefits or non economic related benefits both. Then,the teacher or the school will have possible to persuade whose students to raise learning interest when they choose to learn in the

school.

How to let the student to feel the school can give good economic related or non-economic related benefits to satisfy the student future career plan successful development need persuasively and attractively? It will need to include psychological factor to influence its students to raise learning interest when they are studying in the school in whose whose learning expereince stage. I assume that every student will learn hardly when the school can persuade its students can believe that they must earn good career benefit when they can follow the school's discipline to learn hardly in whose whole learning stage in the school.

Therefore, one successful persuasive teaching method can influence or persuade the students choose to learn hardly . Usually, in general students need not expect to waste learning time and money to chose one poor teaching quality of school to study. If they can not achieve good examination resultes or they need increase long time to extend their graduation time, then they will feel waste money and time loss to choose the wrong or unsuitable school to study. It is one rational either positive or negative learning feeling when one student gain good or bad examination result consequently.

Hence, one successful school must let students to have confidence , it can raise good quality teaching method to let them to study as well as it can provide good learning environment to let them to feel safe, enjoyable , attractive , persuasive learning attitude when they go to school to enter the classroom to learn every day. So, the school must need to let all students to feel they won't waste money and time economic or non-economic related losses when they choose the school to learn, if the school expected to persuade its students to choose to learn easily.

Therefore, learning behavioral economic theory explains that student individual learning interest whether whose interest is raised or not which has been related to influence whether he/she feels his/her learing attitude or learning behavior will bring either waste learning time and money loss or not in whole learning career in the school consequently. Usually, every student won't expect to waste his/her learning time and money if he/she can not earn economic or non-economic related benefits to his/her future job career.

It implies that non-wasted time and money psychological factor brings to the student feeling to learn that will be one man economic factor to influence the student chooses to do hard learning behavior. For example, when a young age student does not choose to go to the school, because he/she does not conern whether he/she will earn a better life in the future. He/she must be persuaded to feel the school is fun now or is given no better opinion to compare the school. Hence, the school needs to let the young age student to feel there are not other schools opinions are better to compare to the school as well as the school can provide attractive teaching method to let the student to feel more fun to lern when he/she chooses the school to learn. Therefore, providing fun learning environment and fun teaching method both factors will be one important to encourage the stdent to learn hardly. The particular educational outcomes worth encouragement, such as attainment, attendance, and homework issues of these educational components will must be achieved fun learning feeling to let the student to whose learning interest encouragingly or persuasively. So, fun learning environment can bring the student individual learning interest in possible. It means that if the student does not feel fun to learn when he/she goes to the school to learn every day. Then, he/her poor fun learning feeling will discourage he/she feels why he/she needs to go to school to attend every lesson to learn in classrooms hardly. So, fun learning environment. fun teaching method, hun homework, fun learning content etc. teaching related components factor will encourage every student likes to go to school to listen every lesson hardly every day in possible. Present-biased learning behavior has important implications in education. Doing fun homeowrks, studying for fun exams, researching fun colleges or potential opportunities for financial aid and completing applications all involve educational cost which will let any students choose to weigh the future learning cost to evaluate which school will be possible to bring educational loss spending cost to evaluate whether he/she ought to choose which school to study in preference. Hence, it explains that the student will consider whether the school can prvide fun learning environment and fun learning subjects or courses to let them to choose to study and whether he/she can feel fun teaching method to satisfy whose learning need. Then, the school will be possibe increased successfuly chance to let the student to choose it to enrol to study in preference. Moreover, attractive courses choices, providing fun learning environment, providing good and fun teaching method quality , fun teaching book contents choices to let students to study etc. thesefactors will encourage students to raise learning interect successfully.

However, any schools need focue only on salient factors , it implies that even simple optimizing decisions may not always be made. So, with a better understanding of student individual fun learning environment and fun teaching method learning need and fun courses teaching learning contents , subjects choices etc. these factors will possible bring knowledg to design more effective learning policies and improve student individual learning outcomes.

Moreover, improving student learning attitude factor is also important to raise whose learning interest. For example, by reading motivational passages or watching tagic movies which can encourage students to focus on positive identifies related to learning and intellectual curiosity may be one approach a growing evidence suggests that many students and parents are not fully informed about education costs , future economic and non-economic related benefits and options. It is possible related to whose low-income family backgrounds and poor learning attitude both factors. So, if the family was one high income family, it will have possible to influence whose sons or daughts to build good learning attitude. When they have good learning attitude and good family growing relatonship . Theb, they will raise learning interest , due to they had built from good learning attitude when they are living in one good family relationship environment. In special, when the family is one low income family and low educational level background, parents will beed to work, so they will neglect to teach whose sons or daughters to know whether they ought how to learn easily, which wil be one correct or right learning attitude to learn by themselves successfully. They will neglect and lack useful educational recommendation to compare education cost, future economic and non-economic eduational benefits and learning attitude and opinion methods and the suitable courses and teaching books contents opinions to let whose their sons and/or daughters to know how to learn effectively by themselves, instead of school teaching method. So, these students' parents' lacking useful learning recommendation or negligent education learning recommendaton behaviors which will also cause the low income family students to build " discouraged hard learning attitude" to let them to raise interest to learn any more new knowledge persuasively. Even, due to the non-educational behavioral opinion of pre-school decision making opinion, if the parents discovered that the school is one suitable school to let their sons and/or daughters to learn persuasively or attratively in order to let they can earn good examination resultsor pass subjects more easily. Then, these disappointed parents and low grade examination result of students will feel need to learn more hardly if they are still not improving theire grade when they feel that they had been studying hardly in the school. Consequently, it will bring more negative learning emotion to the students and families. Hence, disappointing or poor or negative learning attidude or emotion to the student's feeling , this factor must not raise the student individual interest to learn in the school. Otherwise, positive or good learning emotion or attitude will influcence the student to raise learning interest to continue to learn in the school consequently. hence, schools ought not neglect to improve students to build positive learning emotion or attitude habitually in order to raise whose interest to learn in the school more easily.

Can effective school management behavior method raise student learning interest

How and why effective school management behavior can influence the school's student individual to raise learning interest. What is the relationship to bring student individual learning interest to be raised between the student and the school? An effective school mangement behavior can make the function bring that teaching and learning take place in the most effective way. In managing school's systems have to operate so that a whole range of social, intellectural and emotional activites can evolve and develop (pay foot et , 1989). It seems that an effective school management system can change student individual to do a range of positive social, intellectual and emotion activities in order to raise whose learning interest.

Therefore, innovating the traditional education system, changing many aspects of school structures, systems and organization as well as recognizing that the more teachers at all levels in a school's hierarchy who had management training of some kind, the better is needed to some traditional educational organzations. Any educational organizations need have good management functions ,which include: setting the right aims and objectives, planning how a goal will be achieved, organizing available educational resources (how teaching time arrangement, how to select teachers and clerical staffs, homework, how revision time allocation, how educational material opinions, e.g. computers facilities, classrooms number and design method and teaching environment, lecture hall seats number, tables and chairs number, library teaching book lending supplies number etc. resources arrangement) . Therefore, the school can be economically achieved in a planned way, controlling the teaching process (i.e. ensuring that the goal is schieved, e.g. raising learning interest to every individual student when he/she is learning at classrooms, reducing the students fail exam and/or test result number.

In fact, if the school expects it can be one real teaching organization, if the school can arrange internal and external structures effectively. Then, the school let students to have more confidence to choose the school to study. Internal structures include: class organizing, sibject choice organizinf, departments organizing, responsibility arranging. Otherwise , external structures include: admission numbers, numbers on raising salary scales, schol budget, leaving ages, staturory length of the school day, arragement methods of appraisal etc. Hence effective school management system can bring more confidence to the student to choose to the school to study and it can encourage him/hse to raise learning interest effectively.

So, it seems that student learning interest has close relationship to concern how the school manages its organization. Because good school management can influence its internal and external teaching reasources how to allocate to use and manage effectively. For example, good classroom teaching environment can influence students to feel easily, an teaching book library can have enough different topic teaching book to let students to borrow to read, or it has enough comouter facilities to let students to find any reading data from internet conveniently. Then , they will be influenced to raise learning interest more easily, because the school has one attractive and fun learning environment to let its students to learn.

Therefore, an effective school management system can influence its students to raise more interest to learn in order to influence they choose to do learning behavior to study more harder in homes or schools. How to bring one effective school management system to infuence students to feel? I shall indicate the main factors as below:

The first factor is one effective school management system needs have an effective hierarchy of headteachers, deputy heads, heads of department different effective organizing systems. It aims to achieve more directing, controlling and commanding to any department leaders to manage themselves departments more easily.

One educational organization's hierarchical pyramid can indicate such as: a headteacher manage or leads one deputy or more than one deputys on the top level, the middle level will include one deputy or more than one deputy manager(s) or lead(s) in one department head or more than one department heads. Next, the middle level will include one department head or leads more than one teacher at the low level. However, any school organization expects to manage or lead themselves schools effectively. They need to organize in such a way that they will try to achieve effective reaults and make every effort to maintain good relationships between those who work in these departments.

Consequently, when the school can have effective hierarchical structure to manage all different teaching staffs to do whose individual teaching behavior effectively. Then, it will bring positive emotion influence to every teacher to teach whose students more effectively. Hence, every classroom students' learning attitude will enjoy to bring more learning feeling when they are real raised learning interest from their teachers' teaching method influence persuasively.

The second factor is that each staff group participation. It will be the school's staff group participation behavioral factor, how it influences every classroom overall students' learning behaviors to be positive learning emotion or attitude when they (every classroom overall students) are listening their every teacher indiviual teaching in every lession in every the classroom. It is important to find out who participates a lot and why, as well as why someone, e.g. teacher contributes every little to the classroom students.

For example, it is because of fear, disagreement or disinterest, the group of teachers may under have useful point to make. So, a group should ideally encourage all its participates to contribute to any discussions and decison making. This issue of participation is one that group leaders have to consider very carefully.

In fact, influence and participation to every teaching group are not always the same. Some teaching staffs who tell a lot may not always be listen to . Others who are quiet and speak very little can, when they do speak, capture, the attention of everyone. If this is the case then whoever participates may alter and change depending on who has influence at a specific time and who needs certain individuals to speak and support his or her particular cause. The final factor is that the school needs to know how the stykes to be influenced to every teaching group. Influence can take may forms, it can be both positive and negative. It can either to support or co-operation of others or refuse or nor support or co-operation of others. How this happen with a teaching group can be autocratic teaching colleagues who will attempt to impose their will on the teaching group by movement towards directions in which they eagerly support everyone and everything and try to avoid conflict at any cost and those who is influenced by distancing themselves from the whose procedings influence others to do the same. Hence, in a effective teaching group , the teacher's header, e.g. deputy or headteacher ,the middle level staffs or the top level staffs will need to manage themselves every teaching group, e.g. each classroom teacher individual teaching behavior is more easily and effectively. When the classroom teacher can have good teaching performance to teach his/her students in the lesson. Then, he/she can raise every lesson's student individual learning interest more easily or persuasively.

The final school management factor is that, what is the most suitable or right school ethos and whose school aims to the school. If the school chose the most right school aims, then it can able to develop attitudes which won't only help pupils to learn more effectively or raise their interet to learn only, even , it can shoe them the technique of learning and how to continue to want to learn. I shall recommendation that these characteristics of the most suitable or right school aims in order to achieve effectiveness and a positive ethos the following characteristics will help as below:

An effective and powerful leadership, the deputy head needs to be involved in all major decisions, all teachers need to feel that they own those decisons that directly affect them, there to be consistency and continuity throughout the school organization, e.g. in terms of discipline, patterns, homework number and course content test or examination questions contents allocation policies, resource management, subject courses timetable structures etc. teaching sessions need to be structures, matched to pupils' needs, the actual teaching should be intellectually challenging for all pupils, the learning environment of the school whether it will be task -and -work orientated, i.e. every pupil will recognize learning is the norm rather than the exception, there will be lots of communication between teachers and pupils both inside and outside the classroom, record-keeping and assessment are sensible and thorough and are communicated to parents when necessary in a way that they can understand, whether there is a positive learning climate where emphasis is placed on praise rather then criticism control in classrooms is firm , but fair, with children being treated as individuals, any teaching or resource allocation , teaching time allocation activities whether are organized to take place outside the classroom and away from the school. This is a means of offering pupils wider experiencs and a way of putting. The academic content of the curriculum into a different content.

Consequently, how to organize the school in effective way factor which will be one main influential factor to influence teachers to do positive or negative teaching behavior to persuade whose students can raise more learning interest in classrooms. So, it seems that teacher indivivudal positive or negative teaching emotion or attitude will influence their teaching performance or teaching behavior to improve to be better in order to raise the school's students' learning interest more easily or persuasively.

Improving financial education effectiveness through behavioral economic to raise student individual learning interest

How any why does improve financial education effective behavior which can raise student individual learning interest? How to innovate application of lessons from psychology to a financial education programme which can raise student individual learning interest effectively? I shall apply student learning behavioral economic methods to explain why and how improving financil education can be effective to raise student individual learning interest.

The standard economic approach to financial education argues that financial consumers will behave in their own best interests of the financial market is perfectly competitive. In fact, in educaton industry, education consumers, e.g. student parents do not have enough all the knowledge and information concerns what where their sons and/or daughts ought need to choose which subject(s) to study which are(is) the most suitable their interest and effort to learn, whether what the school fee budget level is the most reasonable, what the course contents are the most effective to let their sons or/and daughts to learn easily etc. different related educational institutes information questions to have enough time to prepare to gather these information in order to compare which school is the best or the most suitable school choce for their son and/or daught to study more easily. Thus, of the student consumer's parents can have enough fully information concerns to education institutions how to assist them to make the most reasonable school choice making decision more accurate.

What are the differences between Asia and Western liberal studies teaching aims and influences

What is the meaning of " liberal studies" ? Liberal studies subject is related to " liberal act", " liberal education" or " general education", in asia or foreign education system. Liberal means acts or sciences, pursuits, occupations whether which is suitable to persons of superior social status, general intellectual enlargement, it is required of technical or professional training.

Paris and Kimball (2000, 144) defines liberal education means that becoming multicultural, eveluating general education and integration, rather than specialization, promoting the commonweal and citizenship, regarding all levels of education or belonging to a common enterprise, reconceiving teaching as stimulating learning and inquiring, promoting the formation of values and the practice of service and employing assessments.

However, some educators argue to bring different vieww points, they feel liberal studies subject does not only mean arts or sciences. They remark that students in the USa lack the broad foundation of knowledge necessary to cope with post industrial society and maintains that there is a need to develop " courses in the humanities, social science and natural sciences that challenge young people to think synthetically and to understand that the essence of education is the courage and ability to make value judgements.

Hence foreign high schools hope liberal studies can train every student to make personal judgement and analysis ability to decide to make any matters more accurate. Also, it explains why foreign high schools permit high school students to select this liberal studies subject to study. Because foreign high schools feel taht this subject is one free choice interesting subject. Some students won't feel that teaching hoe to make personal judgement and analysis , which will not bring useful knowledge to help them to find any jobs to do or they feel that social any occupations won't need to learn liberal studies knowledge or this subject does not relate to help their career development.

Otherwise, in some asian countries , such as Hong Kong , high schools feel that this subject is not only interesting subject, it is art subject. These Hong Kong schools feel this liberal studies can develop in learners open mindedness, rational thinking, citizenship, multiculturalism and the ability to make value judgements and it should also promote the integration of useful knowledge and involve the use of enquiry for teaching. So, it explains that why Hong Kong high schools must need have this liberal studies subject to be taught and students must be learnt to pass in order to enrol any universities to study successfully.

Hong kong high schools feel this subject must help students to be trained to make more accurate judgement and accurate analysis mind and skills. If the Hong Kong high schools have mone this subject to be taught to learn its students to learn. Then, the high school students can not confirm or ensure they own accurate judgement and analysis skills or abilities to prepare their further occupation development or carrer development successfully. For example, recently Hong Kong many high school students who are persuaded to force to crash Hong Kong government legislative building and Hong Kong police force building as well as they bring crowd to stay on driving roads to cause traffic jam, even any buses, taxies, cars, lorries , trams etc. transportation tools can not be driven to go through any driving roads absolutely.

Hence, this liberal studies subject can bring negative influence to Hong Kong liberal studies learning students to encourage them to do the anti-social behaviors when themselves feel dissatisfactory or sad or unhappy to Hong Kong government's policy implementation nowadays. It reflects or implies that Hong Kong liberal studies subject teachers had persuaded or they had encouraged these Hong Kong high school students to to anti-social behaviors easily. If Hong Kong high schools chose liberal studies subject was on select (choice) subject or withdraw this subject must be taught in schools. Then, I believe that Hong Kong students won't choose to do anti-social behaviors to complaint their Hong Kong government more easier, because Hong Kong liberal studies high school teachers ' anti-socail psychology will influence how their teaching attitudes to be taught to their students as well as how they teach anti-society or anti-Hong Kong government knowledge to let their students to learn or their teaching behaviors will influence their students ought do anti-social behaviors, it is right after this liberal studies course is finished. Consequently, their Hong Kong students will raise anti-social feeling and they will be persuaded or encouraged to do anti-social behaviors to complaint their Hong Kong government , such as recently many Hong Kong young people had planned to attack or damage Hong Kong legislative building and Hong Kong police force headquarter building. Also, their anti-social behaviors are implemented consequently and it causes Hong Kong polices need to threaten these Hong Kong young peoples' anti-social behaviors. So, liberal studies subject may influence Hong Kong students to choose to do anti-social behaviors more easily. I think that Liberal education does that by teaching students to become lifelong learners who are their own best teachers. It enables them to take intellectual risks and to think laterally -- to understand how the humanities, the arts and the sciences inform, enrich and affect one another. By connecting diverse ideas and themes across the academic disciplines, liberal arts students learn to better reason and analyze, and express their creativity and their ideas.

Why does liberal studies become a core subject to Hong Kong high schools? In addition to liberal studies , there are three other core subjects in Hong Kong educational system, such as Chinese language, English language and mathematics in Hong Kong education system. Traditionally, languages have been considered as tools not only for communication, but also for learning, such as english language must be learnt to Hong Kong students, because they need to write english to do their homeworks, assignments, they need to listen english when their teachers choose to use english language to teach their students in classrooms as well as they also need to read any english books. So, english subject must be one essential subject to be taught to any Hong Kong primary, secondary, and university students nowadays.

But, why will liberal subject be a core subject in Hong Kong schools? Before 2009, liberal studies subject was never a core subject at any level in Hong Kong, but when Hong Kond education reforms which started at the end of the 20 th century. One of the key elements is curriculum reform, in relation to which the curriculum development council published learning to learn life learning and whole-person development (curriculum development council , 2001).

Hong Kong education system began to promote a willingness to learn throughout one's life and the capacity to engage in such learning in one of the key aims of the curriculum reform. In most cases, Hong Kong educators felt lifelong leaning involves learning by oneself, outside schools and institutes and in this sense it is closely related to independent learning. They also felt that liberal studies subject compares other subjects, it may be unique in its potential contribution to train Hong Kong students to raise in order to achieve aim to own more independent learning capability and lifelong learning as Hong Kong students and expected to engage in a variety of enquires and carry out an independent project.

So, Hong Kong eduators believed liberal studies subject can bring the good idea of whole-person development, promotion of moral and civic education and it is a response to the useful of learning knowledge to train Hong Kong young people to achieve one perfect whole-person development before they enter Hong Kong society to work further. So , it explains that why Hong Kong high students must need liberal studies subject to be a core subject to be taught to let students to learn as well as they must pass this subject if they expected to enrol to any Hong Kong universities to study successfully further. Otherise, foreign high schools feel this liberal studies subject is only one select (choice) subject, because they feel thay some students won't have much interest to learn this subject, it is only common act subject and it is not same to psychological subject in universities or it is one occupational choice (select) subject in relation to raise whole-person development to every student absolutely. So, it explains why it brings the difference between select (choice 0 and essential subject of liberal studies learning to asian and foreign high school students nowadays.

In Hong Kong liberal studies subject learning aim aspect, Hong Kong educators believe that liberal studies subject can bring these advantages to young people. They believe that liberal studies subject will foster students' capacity for life-long learning, so that it can train them to face the challenges of the future with confidence. Moreover, lifelong learning is not limited to a set of independent learning skills, but is a culture, such as Chinese culture of how one should position oneself in our changing world. So, Hong Kong liberal studies subject main teaching aim may include: Training every student's personal lifelong learning attitude, building Chinese lifelong learning culture, awareness of continue learning is essential, active relevant ,and continupus, training them to apply high technological learning tools, training their learning attitudes are influenced on focus is on the how more than the what, training they demonstrate information literacy, inquiries are nurtured and training them to take responsibility for their learning. So, Hong Kong educators expect to train or build Hong Kong students have good learning attitudes and building Chinese lifelong learning culture to Hong Kong next generation.

However, Hong Kong liberal studies subject aims to help students to understand issues faced by society and to respect different opinions. Liberal studies teachers expect to train their these skills to be improved, such as generic skills, these are a high demand for generic skills in Hong Kong society, in which the economy is knowledge based liberal studies brings great emphasis on the development of such skills for meeting Hong Kong societal needs. The idea that generic skill affect performance in a wide range of functioning is by no means a new concept. Liberal studies is expected to be taught how good cooperating to do any tasks or projects or assignments, when students need to cooperate with colleagues in complex environment of work. Generic skills can not operate without knowledge, such as building s bridge needs have engineering knowledge or writting an essay needs have vocabilary and grammer of the language knowledge. Hence, generic skills are supported to be transferable skills which effort performance in many.

Also, liberal studies subject can teach communication skills, when a classroom learning and teaching activity is needed to group discussion in classroom as well as when students are insolved in enquiry or an issue , they will usually work in small groups and so group discussion becomes essential . So, liberal studies subject can be taught to train students how to understand of turn-raking, the ability to identify others' viewpoints and an appreciation that every one's views should be respected most easily. It can train collaborative skills, how to help students to engage effectively in tasks and teamwork. Because group work can be used to develop not only students' communication skills, but also their ability to cooperate effectively with others. When Hong Kong students can learn liberal studies subject, then when they explore on issue in groups , they can have more confidence to work with classmates in making decisions on, for example, how to analyze the sorts of information needed to finish any tasks more easily and how it can be collected and organized more easily. Also, liberal studies subject can train students how to negotiate and argue move towards a consensus more easily. Liberal studies subject can train students to raise critical thinking skills, such as how to help them to draw out meaning from given data or statements, generate and evaluate arguments, and train them to make more accurate judgement to finish any matters or tasks more easily and effectively and efficiently. This is the teaching aims of liberal studies subject in Hong Kong high schools nowadays.

However, Hong Kong educators also believe liberal studies subject can train these skills to high school students, such as problem solving skills, how to understand the problem to note the existing data and constraints and see what is needed to solve it more easily, how to formulate a plan, carry out the plan and check it by confirmation of each relevant test at each stage and to check the solution to see if it can be improved more easily, creatie skills, liberal studies can engage students in investigation in groups to develop and evaluate solutions to various problems through such activities, it is possible that liberal studies can train students learn how to create a creative environment to provide them to raise the more ability to generate original ideas and solve problems more easily, liberal studies lessons can train students hoe to see, analyse, manage easily and present information critically in an intelligently information age and a digitised world.

However, the aim difference of the liberal studies subject between Asian and Western is that Western liberal studies subject is only concentrate on art interesting aspect, e.g. focusing on social and personal psychological research, music , historical , social science knowledge researchs. Otherwise, Asian liberal studies subject focuses on whole-person development aspect, e.g. training students how to improve itself country residents' quality of life, learning how the country's residents participate in political and social affairs with rights and responsibilities with respect to the rule of law, learning how to demonstrate a sound understanding of the key idea, concepts and terminologies of the subject as well as developing the capacity to construct knowledge through enquiring into contemporary issues with affect themselves, their society, their nation, the human world and physical environment, learning how to reflect on the development of Asian youngers' own multiple identifies, value systems and world views with respect to personal experiences, social and cultural contexts and the impacts of developments in science, technology and globalization, learning how to identify the values of different views and judgements on personal and social issues and how to apply critical thinking skills, creativity and different perspectives in making decisions and judgements on issues and problems at both how to present arguments clearly and demonstrate respect for evidence, and open-mindedness and tolerance towards the views and values held by other people, learning how to develop skills related to enquiry learning , including self-management skills, problem-solving skills, communication skills, information processing skills, and skills in using information and communication technology, learning how to carry out self-directed learning which includes the processes of selling goals, making and implementating drawing conclusions, reporting findings and conducting evaluation skills, learning how to demonstrate an appreciation for the values of their own and other cultures, and for values, and be committed to becoming responsible and conscientious citizen in themselves countries.

Given the global leadership of American higher education, and the global economy's demands for flexible, adaptable employees, undergraduate liberal education is more than relevant. It remains one of our country's great assets. Is it for everyone? Of course not. But for those who pursue liberal arts education, it can be life transforming.Thus, it explains although western countries and asia countries both have liberal studies subject to be taought in high schools and universities , but liberal studies subject is only select (choice) subject to western countries' high schools because this subject is not focus in whole-persone development, it is only interesting subject, such as any act subjects in western countries' educational system. Otherwise, asia countries consider liberal studies subject is one essential subject in high schools because asia countries feel it can train every youngers' whole person development skills to prepare their further possible unpredictive any challenge facing solving ability when they work in society. So, the difference views of this subject is that liberal studies subject is only one short time interesting learning subject to let students to choose to study in western high schools, but otherwise, this subject is one long time whole -person development learning knowledge to prepare their further social work development life period or career period. Hence, it explains that short time learning interest view and long time whole-person development view both to which can influence that whether liberal studies subject is one essential subject or one select (choice) subject between asia and western high schools nowdays.

The differences between Asia and Western Liberal studies

advantages and disadvantages

What Is Liberal Studies? Liberal studies, also known as liberal arts, comprises a broad exploration of social sciences, natural sciences, humanities, and the arts. If you are interested in a wide-ranging education in humanities, communication, and thinking, read on to find out about the educational and career possibilities in liberal studies. Schools offering Liberal Arts degrees can also be found in these popular choices. People often assume "liberal arts" is a political term. As it's used in academia it's closer to the idea of broadening the mind and "liberating" it from parochial divisions and unthinking prejudice. It encourages the questioning of assumptions and reliance on facts as well as an understanding that even facts can be interpreted differently through different lenses. Ideally, it enables individuals to gather information, interpret it, and make informed decisions on a wide variety of topics.It's not just the "soft" subjects like English and sociology that constitute a liberal arts education. People often talk about STEM (Science, Technology, Engineering and Math) courses, as totally separate from "liberal arts" courses. They think of "science" as "real" in a way that anthropology or art history are not: an atom is an atom, after all. But scientific phenomena are also subject to interpretation and debate as they are observed and theories are created and tested. Even a cursory knowledge of evolutionary theory or the light as wave/particle debate demonstrates that point.

The "hard" sciences are ways of seeing the world and trying to understand how it works just as much as psychology or political science are. A good liberal arts curriculum puts students in touch not just with ways of interpreting the world around us but also with the fact that the world can be "interpreted" in the first place. Ultimately, it tries to help us understand our place in it and our relationships with each other.

Degree Levels Bachelor's, master's and Ph.D. Concentrations American Studies, Humanities, International Affairs, Social and Public Policy Common Courses Writing, Social Foundations, Environmental Studies, Global Cultures Online Availability Full- and part-time online programs available. You may be required to complete some courses on-campus. Median Salary (2018) $78,470 (Postsecondary Teachers), Job Outlook (2016-2026) 15% (Postsecondary Teachers)U.S. Bureau of Labor Statistics (BLS) .

What is a Liberal Studies Program?

Liberal studies programs culminate in associate's or bachelor's degrees. Classes in anthropology, art, music, ethnic studies, psychology, sociology, literature, philosophy, communications and most other departments in the humanities will count towards a liberal studies degree. Some possible career options with this degree include elementary school teacher, retail store manager, minister or a public relations specialist. The table below outlines some general requirements for these career options. Undergraduate degree programs in liberal studies and liberal arts involve core and elective coursework in a variety of subjects, including history, cultural studies, art, philosophy, religion, literature, and the natural sciences. In general, the goal of a liberal studies program is a strong, basic foundation of knowledge and skills that will support an array of careers and interests. Some programs allow you to develop your own path of coursework based on your interests, while others offer concentrations in areas such as early education or performing arts.

It is one interesting question: Does liberal studies only bring advantages, but it has none any disadvantages. It seems to research how to live in Mars planet destination question. Although, human provides suitable living envioronment to let us to live, instead of our earth. Research Mars planet to live, it is one worth research , but we can not guarantee whether Mras planet will bring what disadvantages to let us to live in possible, when ww really live in Mars planet in future one day, the disadvantages may include, for example, whether Mars planet's weather environment is suitable to human to live in long time, during ir is very cool at night or very hoe in some places, the trouble is the pole areas get as cold as -195 degree and are prone to storms that make landing even harder. It is also not a very exciting place, the northern plains of Mars are pretty that and boring. The equational region mostly stays above -100 degree and can reach 20 degree. It also has more sunlight that astronauts could harvest for solar power, rearely gets storms and has all sorts of interesting terrain to explore. But it does not seem to have much, if any accessible water, or whether Mars planet's lands can be built in stable. Any houses won't be damages from unpredictable bad geographical environment influence easily. Mars planet travellers are about to face the most dangerous part of their journey, the trouble with landing on Mars is that its atmosphere is almost non-existent, it is 160 times less dense than Earth's , on average . This means , but because gravity on Mars is stronger than that on the moon, we would need a lot more boosters. This means we will probably need a combination of boosters and something to create drag.

Hence, once Mars researchers are down, the explorers will be struking around for a whike . Even if they are not establishing a permanent settlement. They will have to wait months at a minimum for Earth and Mars to come into a alignment again, so they can travel home in a matter of months rather than years. There is no visiting Mars without setting up a base.

Why I concern that liberal studies subject whether it can bring advantages only, it seems to Mars planet living research whether Mars can bring more advantages to let us to live to replace Earth. This question seems to ask whether liberal studies can assist students to raise any skills or abilities to be trained to learn other subjects more easily, or training their judgement, analysis abilities to be raised or training to be whole person development absolutely in order to achieve these all positive advantages absolutely or this subject can not bring positive advantages to assist students to learn any other subjects more easily absolutely. In general, in a liberal studies curriculum brigs these benefits, students sharpen their reading and writing skills by completing research papers. You also practice verbalizing your ideas through classroom discussions and learn to develop multiple perspectives. Other skills developed include: Critical and analytical thinking, effective communication, reasoning and problem solving. What careers that students can attempt to seek after they had graduated liberal studies degree in university? A liberal studies education doesn't prepare you for only one specific career; instead, the skills you learn in a liberal studies program can be beneficial in multiple professions. Solid writing and communication skills are paramount to most positions, and the critical-thinking skills you learn can be applied to any field that requires analytical thought, such as business or education. Other possible career areas include the following: Sales and marketing,

nonprofit organization director, journalist,
education administration, politician, college recruiter,
urban planner/city manager etc. positions. Also, liberal
studies graduated students could choose a writing-
intensive career as a columnist, editor or research assistant.
Businesses often hire liberal studies graduates as customer
service and relations personnel, coordinators and
consultants, who then may advance towards management
and executive positions. Many lobbyists, politicians,
creative writers, speech writers, journalists and archivists
have all started careers with a liberal studies education. A
liberal studies degree can also be applied towards a master's
degree, and a future career in education or a variety of
other fields.

Liberal studies programs offer a way for you to
strengthen almost any career skills you want. The
independent nature of your degree, along with courses in
communications, can help you develop your work ethic
and teamwork skills. Literature and foreign language classes
may enhance your abilities to read and write critically, self-
motivate and speak publicly. Classes in the social sciences
can sharpen your analytical skills, familiarizing you with
data cohorts and statistical models. At a real-world
internship, you'll be given a chance to advance and test
these skills while you learn to network.

According to the U.S. Bureau of Labor Statistics (BLS) there
are a wide variety of careers available to those who pursue a
liberal studies degree and therefore, an equally wide salary
range. For example, a retail store manager makes a median
annual income of $38,310 in 2015, but a public relations
specialist or an elementary school teacher make
considerably more - $56,770 and $54,550, respectively.

However, teachers require licensure in their state of residence and therefore, additional education. The same is true of those who pursue a career in the ministry or clergy - while some denominations only require a bachelor's degree and some on-the-job training, other denominations prefer a master's degree in ministry leadership. Liberal Studies is meant to allow students to develop an open mind through critical thinking. Students are introduced to a host of issues and are then taught to look at the issue from different perspectives. But many teachers force their students to follow a particular writing style or stick to model answers. And most students do so, because they are scared they will be penalised in terms of marks if they don't. This defeats the whole purpose of Liberal Studies. If we are learning to express our opinions, why should we follow model answers?

Such as Hong Kong liberal studies advantages and disadvantages case study, Hong Kong lineral studies is core subject. It aims to link up knowledge of all subjects. HK education proposal is 3 years in junior school, 3 years in senior high school and 4 years in university. It aims to link up knowledge, such as economic, geography. Is it benefit to HK students? What are the advantages and disadvantages of the subject itself brought to HK students? Is it advisable to include liberal studies as a core subject in HK education system in 2008 year on teaching material and teacher's supply preparation aspect?

Liberal Studies is meant to train our critical thinking skills. But when we look at the exam, we don't see how that's implemented. We are asked questions that seem to require fixed answers, according the marking scheme. I always thought the marking scheme was there just for reference, but we are confined to giving the exact ideas provided in the scheme.I think there needs to be better communication between the Hong Kong Examinations and Assessment Authority, the Education Bureau, the markers and the teachers about what exactly they want from the students. Do they want facts, or do they want our opinions? They keep saying the subject aims to improve our critical thinking, but I don't feel the current system helps us improve in that area.

I think we need to link the goal to the method by which it is achieved. I believe the failure in doing this is one of the main reasons British and American universities ignore Liberal Studies grades when making offers to students.What the HKEAA led us to believe about Liberal Studies wasn't really the full picture. For a start, there are hidden model answer formats that mean if students misinterpret some words in the question, a heavy penalty is imposed.What's more, students have to think and write unbelievably fast to complete the paper, as there are so many questions. How can students master the skills needed to answer Liberal Studies questions? Our current method of "learning by doing" does not apply to this subject.

Hong Kong some liberal studies students , they feel learning challenges to study this subject. They indicated that the biggest problem with Liberal Studies is that it is an exam-based subject. As such, lots of teachers and students focus more on acquiring the skills necessary to answer the questions than on discussing current affairs. Instead of developing students' interest in current affairs, this only strengthens exam skills. It would be better if Liberal Studies was more coursework-based than exam-based. Otherwise, other some different view point liberal studies students indiated that they feel these challenges concern liberal studies learning thatI don't think it's fair that it is a core subject that is forced upon students. While it is important to have some knowledge of current affairs, we shouldn't be examined on our understanding of social issues. Some students at my school didn't get in to university because they didn't pass this subject at DSE level.

Of course, no reference to free speech is complete without also acknowledging the mechanism by which it is exercised. Social media and technology have been a decidedly mixed blessing in promoting civil discourse. Read the comments section on just about any news story having to do with one of America's top liberal arts schools, and you'll find no shortage of trolls and vitriolic anti-intellectualism.The value of a liberal arts education. they received an outstanding liberal arts education as an undergraduate, and it continues to shape their career and life. They firmly believe liberal education is the best preparation a young person can have for the job market and a rewarding, meaningful life as a citizen of our democracy.

However, HK educators identified some advantages and disadvantages of liberal studies to HK students. The advantages may include; Helping students to build ip own points of view, cultivating students' critical thinking skill, preventing students' single track approach, due to the specialization in secondary subjects, broadening students' knowledge base, increasing students' learning incentive, providing an integration of knowledge of all subjects mutually, providing the future generation with wider knowledge use, independent thinking, creativity in a knowledge oriented society and enabling students to obtain a life long benefits.

But, it also brings disadvantages, they may include: No

definite textbook of liberal studies, leading to strong contrast and confrontation between liberal studies and traditional subjects, it may become a new burden or learning pressure to the student, unfairness may result as there is no standard answer in assessment of liberal studies. Also, many HK educators feel that it is not possible to include liberal studie as core subject, the reasons may include: It lacks cautious plan, housing building on Mars land technological skill, food growing technolgical skill, preventing unpredictive bad weather change on Mars technological skill before the Mars living planning will decide to implement. So, Hong Kong liberal studies disadvantages include , it lacks a comprehensive training of teachers, can not be alloweded to be trained within a limited period of 35 hours. Hence, HK liberal studies teaching implement needs have enough time to research to work out what training best fits teachers, what teaching resources must need to provide. It seems to the Mars living research implementation plan. Before ,any countries need to implement any liberal studies subject , they need to find what weaknesses or challanges they are facing to achieve this liberal studies subject as well as they also need to find any solutions to solve the challanges to threaten the liberal studies subject to be implemented. If they neglect how to solve any challenges they will face to implement liberal studies subject, then they will encounter failure to implement the liberal studies subject to let young people to learn in their schools unsuccessfully.

In conclusion, a liberal arts education can be very frustrating. It forces students to see multiple viewpoints and continually challenge their own. It removes the comfort of assuming there are "right" answers to big questions, that civilization moves in a linear fashion or that facts are facts no matter who looks at them. But it also introduces students to the pleasures of debate and the ever-expanding world of ideas. It opens doors, enabling the mind to go wherever it wants in the pursuit of knowledge and understanding. It bends toward openness instead of containment.In times of great division, the capacity to see others' viewpoints and the imperative to assess one's own become more and more important. A liberal arts education works for us, no matter what our political leanings are. We need it now more than ever.College students who major in the humanities always get asked a certain question. They're asked it so often—and by so many people—that it should come printed on their diplomas. That question, posed by friends, career counselors, and family, is "What are you planning to do with your degree?" But it might as well be "What are the humanities good for?"It is possible that liberal studies can help students to solve whys and hows of human behavior in their daily life more easily.What matters now is not the skills you have but how you think. Can you ask the right questions? Do you know what problem you're trying to solve in the first place? Educator argues for a true "liberal arts" education—one that includes both hard sciences and "softer" subjects. A well-rounded learning experience, he says, opens people up to new opportunities and helps them develop products that respond to real human needs. Summarily, liberal studies can bring students these benefits after their learning experience, such as: 1. To build the concept of "valuable learning" from the various meanings that college students gave to it when they were asked about their opinion of the valuable things they learned in liberal education courses they have taken as part of their curriculum. 2. To approach to the ways students think and feel about liberal education, so those educational approaches with greater learning potential could be strengthened. The instrument used to collect students? 3. Training students how to collect, classify, analyze and interpret multiple answers that students gave any questions allowed a better understanding of the impact of the liberal education courses.

Chapter 3

Skill training talent human method

Skill is an ability or effort that you need to put time to develop. Talent refers to an inborn and special ability you own it. So, when one person can attempt to learn ths kind of skill. It is possible that he can be trained to be talent person. How to Create Effective Skills Training with Career Pathing ? Your company's ability to address the skills gap is going to be the most significant issue facing HR in the next decade. Relying on the recruitment of new hires will no longer be a viable solution. Digital transformation of the workplace means that AI and automation are continually rendering skills obsolete while creating new jobs in the process. As those new roles emerge, the existing talent pool will be insufficient to meet demand. Employers will no longer be able to fall back on their default strategy of hiring new workers.

● How to improve staff skill to be talent labour ?

As the 'future of work' begins to assume a more defined shape, the majority of employers are placing more emphasis on training of their existing talent, but skills development is not moving fast enough to keep up with demand. Ongoing upskilling and reskilling can help to offset the impact on your workforce from these fundamental changes.

Creating personalized development opportunities

When it comes to developing your talent, there is no 'one size fits all' approach. To succeed in today's workplace the following steps are recommended. Your approach must become more personal, placing development at the center of your overall business strategy.

Personalized development opportunities should be offered to enhance skills acquisition. This approach enables you to provide your employees with the tools they need to acquire new skills.

As well as being targeted to the individual, employees should be able to learn in their own time. Technology can help to support this. A further, critical point to note is that learning and development is not exclusively for the C Suite but should be offered to all of your employees.

● Career pathing strategy improve employee individual skill ?

Career pathing provides a clear route into all of these options, enables you to create individual learning programs for all of your employees and offers the following benefits. Employees create their own career paths, which are aligned with your organization's business goals. All employees are guided to understand their own strengths and weaknesses and are empowered to identify key areas for development. They are inspired to work towards vertical or lateral moves within your organization, for example, through job rotation (ie, where employees assume new tasks in a different role for a specified period before they 'rotate' back to their original post). Career pathing enables HR and management to understand and analyze employee aspirations through internal mobility programs and aligns well with your succession planning program. So, career pathing strategy is one kind of good skill to raise staff efficiency or improve performance.

● Strategies learning new skills

Are you a visual learner? Or is your learning style kinesthetic or auditory? I'll tell you a secret: you're none of these. As much as we'd like to believe that we learn better in a certain style, the truth is, these have little impact on our ability to learn.

In an intriguing talk at TEDxUWLaCrosse, Dr. Tesia Marshik shares a startling fact: 40 years of research on learning styles has found that matching teaching styles to learning styles makes no difference at all. In her own experiments, Dr. Marshik found that students learned the same way, regardless of the way material was presented to them.

Another study was a little more blunt in its judgments:

1. Learning from technological channel

The contrast between the enormous popularity of the learning-styles approach within education and the lack of credible evidence for its utility is, in our opinion, striking and disturbing. For example, if you're trying to learn a new language, don't just read the textbook. Watch TV shows, listen to music, and converse with a native speaker through a language exchange app. Learners can apply internet to learn any kinds of new kowledge easily.

One main reason why "learning styles" don't work is that we learn things in terms of meaning. Finding meaning in our learning is the key. A 1973 study by Chase and Simon illustrates this well. In the first part of the test, amateur and expert chess players were shown a chessboard arrangement from a game in progress and asked to recall the position of the pieces. While amateurs players could barely recall any of positions, the experts were able to recall most of them. The experts see the strategy, the meaning behind why the pieces are where they are.

In the second part, experts and amateurs were shown boards with the chess pieces arranged at random and asked to recall them. Both groups performed about equally. This time, the experts couldn't find any real connection or meaning in the way the pieces are arranged.

2. Learning from life experience

The same goes for learning. We all learned various facts and figures in school but how many of those do we actually remember? Only the information that was meaningful to us, that we've been able to connect to our own life and experiences. If you try to force yourself to just memorize random facts, you're likely to forget them. Remember all those times you tried to memorize formulae without understanding their relevance? In order to make your learning stick, it's important to make real life connections and see how it fits in the larger scheme of things.

3. learning by attempting doing.

Humans are natural learners—and we learn best when we perform the tasks we're trying to learn. No matter how good your grades were at college, most of your learning takes place once you enter the workplace and start applying what you've learned. Let's say you're trying to learn SEO. Don't invest all your time in learning the jargon and theory—dive in as soon as you can to master the skill through trial and error. Start a blog. Write a few posts. Find out for yourself what works and what doesn't. The more you do it, the more you learn.

Better yet, build new habits to enforce your new skills. Start small and reward yourself to start building a pattern of behavior that will reinforce what you're learning.

4. Learning by study

Aspiring writers hear over and over that the best way to write better is to read a lot of books, especially the classics. Why? Because they'll learn a lot more by studying the writing styles of great writers, than they would by taking a course on writing. Let's take this advice a step further. While studying the greats is essential, it is more of a passive exercise. In order to gain from it, you need to apply that learning to your own work as well. One way to do this is to mimic experts until you eventually develop your own style and technique. Benjamin Franklin taught himself to write this way, as he shares in his autobiography:

I took some of the papers (from The Spectator magazine), and, making short hints of the sentiment in each sentence, laid them by a few days, and then, without looking at the book, try'd to compleat the papers again, by expressing each hinted sentiment at length, and as fully as it had been expressed before, in any suitable words that should come to hand. On comparing his work with the originals, he found where he was lacking, and started turning the tales into poems and then back again. This is how he learned to express himself better. This form of learning can be applied to any skill, be it writing, speaking another language, or even sports. Compare your work with that of experts in your field and you will notice areas that need improvement. Then, refer back to step 3 and keep practicing your skills. You will notice the difference.

5. Learning from past what your teacher tought

One of the more surprising ways you can learn a new skill is to teach it to someone else. Much research has been done on this phenomenon, but one study illustrates it particularly well. In the study, two sets of participants study the same passage, with different expectations. One group was expected to teach it later, the other one expected a test on it. At the end, both groups were eventually tested on the material. Guess which group did better? Yep—the one that expected to teach it.

Why is this such an effective way to learn? Because when we learn with the intention to teach, we break the material down into simple, understandable chunks for ourselves. It also forces us to examine the topic more critically and thoroughly, helping us to understand it better. You don't have to be an education major to use this trick. Try explaining what you're learning to friends or coworkers. If you're learning a new business software or skill, ask your boss if you can make a presentation to your team about it. See if you can field all their questions. Write regular blog posts or make vlogs while you're learning. See if you're able to express what you learn in simple words. The results might surprise you.

6. Learning from spend more time to practise things you feel difficulties

Practice in itself is great, but if you're practicing things you know well, you're doing it wrong. In order to excel at any skill, you need to push yourself out of your comfort zone and practice things you aren't good at. This is known as deliberate practice, and was popularized by Anders Ericsson. Ericsson and his team studied expert athletes, violinists, and memory champions and found that they spent a lot of time improving areas they were weak. Additionally, they consulted their teachers to find out where exactly they were lacking. Along with spending more time on your weaknesses, Ericsson also emphasizes the importance of concentration while practicing. If you're practicing while your mind is all over the place, you're not getting much out of it. So the next time you sit to practice a new skill, step out of your comfort zone and challenge yourself. Concentrate on whatever is most difficult for you, and with time you'll find you achieve a higher level of overall efficiency.

7. Learning takes frequent breaks

The brain has two modes—focused and diffused. For learning to happen, both modes are equally important. While in focused mode, you're able to learn the nitty-gritties of a problem. In diffused mode, you're better able to see the big picture and bring it all together. You might have noticed this happening in the shower, when you're not focusing on anything in particular, then you suddenly remember a fact that was eluding you, or the solution to a problem. It's important to let your brain relax for a while after a particularly intense session of study or practice, to give it time to connect the dots. One good way to practice this is using the Pomodoro technique, which has you work on a project for 25 minutes, and then give yourself a 5 minute break. After four such sessions (that is, 100 minutes of work, with 15 minutes of break) you take another break for 15-30 minutes. This technique helps to keep your mind invigorated, and ensures you don't suffer mental fatigue. Equally important is learning how to procrastinate productively, so your brain has time to truly recharge itself.

8. Learning from test yourself skill again

We all loved to hate tests in school, but do you know just how effective they are in helping you learn? Turns out testing is one of the best ways to boost learning—even if you're simply practicing on your own, and not taking a high-stakes exam. Testing even beats out methods such as re-reading and reviewing notes when it comes to making sure your learning sticks. An examination of the study techniques of top students by Elevate Education found that while most students re-read notes before exams, top students spend their time solving problems and taking practice exams. Why is testing so effective? Because it takes recall a step further. Recall shows how much of the material you remember. Testing shows you how well you can use what you've learnt. After all, that is the ultimate goal of learning, isn't it?

9. Finding a mentor help

Mentorship is perhaps the quickest way to take your skills to the next level. A mentor helps you navigate your field by offering invaluable perspective and experience. Initially, look to friends, family, and coworkers for an expert in the skill you're trying to learn. If you come up with no one, start branching out your search to your larger community and industry. When reaching out to experts, describe what you have to offer, rather than what you will gain. For example, maybe you could manage their social media accounts or help write their website content. Whatever services you can offer, be sure to let them know.

All of aboves are skill learning method to help foolish person to be clever or talent person. So, it seems that learning skill may be one kind of good method to become talent person.Becoming talent human encountering difficulties What are the difficulties to the person who hopes to be talent person ? I shall indicate as below:

● How to solve talent management challenges and difficulties?

Firstly, we need to know what talent management means and what difficulties we shall encounter in talent managment process. What is Talent Management? Talent management is defined as the methodically organized, strategic process of getting the right talent onboard and helping them grow to their optimal capabilities keeping organizational objectives in mind. The process thus involves identifying talent gaps and vacant positions, sourcing for and onboarding the suitable candidates, growing them within the system and developing needed skills, training for expertise with a future-focus and effectively engaging, retaining and motivating them to achieve long-term business goals. The definition brings to light the overarching nature of talent management – how it permeates all aspects pertaining to the human resources at work while ensuring that the organization attains its objectives. It is thus the process of getting the right people onboard and enabling them to enable the business at large.Under the umbrella of talent management, there are a string of elements and sub-processes that need to work in unison to ensure the success of the organization. For example, analyzing the right talent gaps for the present and the future, identifying the right talent pools and best-fit candidates, getting them to join and then optimizing their existing skills and strengths while helping them grow are touch-points that are all equally important.

Talent Management Model

Over the years, there have been multiple models made for talent management that have been created b organization who have felt that they have finally cracked the code on the perfect model. The thing with talent management, however, is that it needs to morph to suit the latest talent trends, digital disruptions, and employee expectations.

● Talent Management Strategy

Talent management is not a mere checklist of requirements that need to be sufficed – it is a strategy that needs careful implementation, regular checks, and continual improvement. The following are the six primary talent management strategies that serve as the pillars of people functions.

1. Detailed job descriptions

A well-informed, detailed job description helps the sourcer, the sourcing software, and the candidate understand the job-role better. Generic job descriptions only serve to confuse all parties involved in the talent acquisition process and lead to a wave of irrelevant applications. Information that must be a part of the job description includes the following:

Job title and location

Overall duties

Skills required

Reporting lines

Tools and equipment used

Salary and benefits

With these, candidates can make an informed decision on whether to apply or not and sourcers get CVs that fit the bill better.

2. Person-organization fit

An employee that does not fit into the organizational culture can neither be the happiest employee nor the most sustainably productive one. While the culture can be difficult to define in words, it is prevalent in actions and quite easy to understand whether a candidate would be a good fit or not. Personal and organizational values need to have a certain degree of overlap for any employee to feel at home within the organization. Without a comfortable person-organization fit, the most amount of time, effort and energy would go into attempts at adjustment. Hiring candidate with the right P-O fit (or PE fit) thus greatly improves the chances of better employee engagement, higher employee satisfaction, and usually better performance.

3. Collaborate-coach-evolve

An important strategy to make talent management more effective involves creating a culture of coaching, mentoring (even reverse mentoring) and collaboration. Constructive feedback goes a long way when it comes to helping employees evolve and develop their skills and expertise. Managing talent is thus also about preparing them for the future of the organization – to be ready for changes down the path and to be able to rely on each other.

4. Reward and recognize right

The process of rewards and recognition forms an important part of the strategy to motivate, engage and manage employees better. This goes beyond financial rewards and bonus packages. Studies point towards the fact that employees often want R&R schemes that motivate them with "prizes" that are most relevant to them as individuals. This is a great opportunity for organizations to show their employees how much they care for them as persons and as integral aspects of the organizational machinery.

5. Opportunities for continuous improvement

Managing talent needs to be put in the context of the future that the organization has envisioned for itself. Thus, employees need to be equipped with the right tools to be able to maximize their own potential. For the continuous improvement of the organization, there needs to be the scope and opportunities for the continuous development of its employees. Moreover, this ensures that the cumulative skills within the organization is updated, upgraded and upscaled.

Talent management involves strategically planning career paths that make sense for every employee. We all tend to work better we know where we are headed and what the next stop is for our careers. This does not entail making empty promises of promotions but rather creating a career map in discussion with the employee, making sure that they relate to it and feel that it is realistic while also providing them with all the necessary tools to make the map a reality. Having a map to follow also improves retention scores since employees then know what they have to look forward to and work towards and can then collaborate effectively to achieve it. So, any organizations may attempt to apply talent management strategy to solve any difficulties when they hope to train talent employees in their organizations more easily.

Skills shortages on developing country market

Future developing countries need to develop their economy, so they need to employ many employees who own technical skills and /or soft skills. What kind of technical skills and/or soft skills , the developing countries' employees who will need to order to raise competiton in local job market ? I shall indicate the developing country

China example. China is one developing country, employers will need different kinds of skillful labors to assist them to develop their businesses. However, China employers will face skillful labour shortage challenge. Although Chinese young age population is high, but many of them do not to be encouraged to learn enough skillful knowledge to fill future new skillful positions. So, the fast speed of training will be important to influence China supply and demand labour market to be more accurately as well as future China's the quality of labour demand number will be influenced to be raised after they have enough training to learn new skills.

How to solve future China skillful shortage of labour? Firstly, nowadays, China employers need to teach their employees to learn how to use and how to operate robotic skills in China's factories. AI robotic has been early developing, so they need to prepare to learn robotic management and operating technical and soft skills in order to satisfy future China factory automation industry development.

China is one world's factory for low-end products to high quality information products, high end technology and services. So, China will need many high skilled workers to assist manufacturers to manufacture many different kinds of products to export or local sale. Moreover, robotic manufacturing skillful workers will also need because robotic will be accepted to assist manual workers to work in China's any factories. This has led to greater demand for labour wirh upgraded skills and competence. So, it seems that China's orkers need to lern any high technological manufacturing knowledge, e.g. learning how to co-operate with robotics to raise productive efficiencies, which will be future many China's manufacturers' skills need intention.

So, when any one of China manufacturer invests robotics to work in its factory . Then, the China manufacturer's labours ought need to know how to co-operate with th robotics to raise productivities and efficiencies. Moreover, these China service industries, e.g. IT, software, accounting, finance, marketing and customer service management, e.g. waiter, property security, shopping center customer service etc. service occupations. In the future, robotics can also used to participate any one of these service industries' part of tasks in order to raise service performance. So, any one of these service industries' employees need to learn how to operate with robotics in order to achieve the most excellent servvice performances to satisfy consumers' needs. So, China service industries labours ought need to learn how to co-operate or manage service natural robotics to work together more efficiently because future China manufacturers will prefer to employ the labours who know how to co-operate and manage and control any service natural robotics more easily and efficiently in order to achieve the most excellent service performance to satisfy customers needs.

Hence, it seems that China manufacturing and service workers need to spend time and effort to learn how to co-operate with manufacturing natural robotics to manufacture any products in factories efficiently or deliver any cargos in warehouses more efficiently or serve customers to let them to feel excellent service performance in restaurants or shopping centers or properties or offices receiption counters. Then, when their China employers apply robotics to participate to work in factories, restaurants, shopping centers, cinemas, offices or properties reception etc. different working places . These low skillful labours will be dismissed easily, due to robotics can replace them to manufacture any products or provide services to satisfy clients' needs in order to let them to fell robotics' performances are more excellent to compare human service labours or their productive efficiencies are more effort to compare workers. So, future China workers need to learn how to cooperate or manage or contol with robotics to work more efficiently, if they do not expect to be dismissed easily.

In the future several occupations have been identified as the most frequent movers between all labour market states. The elementary occupations include: waiters, bar staffs, clearners, catering assistants, construction and security service workers, care workers, sales assistants and general clerks etc. So, the low educational level workers can learn these soft wkills to raise whose professional workering level to prepare to do these above positions in global elementary occupation job market.

The changes of employer were most frequent for IT programmers, doctors, electricians, carpenters, skilled workers in global labour market. These skilled occupations will have manpower shortage supply challenge, due to either people feel the educatonal level is under low. So, there has no many people have interest to know these knowledg to prepare their elementary careers. So, these kinds of low skilled occupations will have not enough human power supply to global labour job market also, the high skilled or educational job support.

Moreover, the high skilled occupations also encounter labour shortage issue. The skills in short supply related to experienced canadidates e.g. five years or more. For example, pharmaceutical , biogharma and food innovation industries. The occupational shortage roles include: Chemists, analytical scientists, product formulation, analytical development for roles in biopharma, quality control analyst includes pharmaco-vigilance, i.e. drug safety roles. The demand for engineering industry aspect which will aos increase the labour shortage includes process and design (research and development, quality control, automation, lean processes) are skillful labours need to help employers to achieve these intentions. They may include raising competitiveness, boosting productivity and skills availability. So, if future these above any one of occupation labours can not achieve these benefits to satisfy their employers' needs. Then, his/her average weekly or hourly wages will be reduced. It means that the unskilled labour under skilled labour wage can not increased more easily, even they own many year working experiences in any one of above these occupations. If the employer feels the labour is unskilled or below skilled level for any one of these occupations in these any one industry aspect, e.g. wholesale and retal , human health, education, accomodaton and food , construction, professional activities, financial service , public administration, and defence, transportation etc. occupations. Then, these industries' unskilled or below skilled level workers' salaries will be lower level to compare the higher skilled workers who work in any one of these industries.

The reason why future employers need to employ skilled labours. One explanation for slow recovery in demand in negative impact on investment is a prolonged period of high unemployment. This is led to job weekers left labour market or became unemployable due. So, future low skillful level will be one important factor to cause unemployment in society as well as nowadays labours ought need consider whether their skills are needed to improve in order to avoid future competition in job market.

2.1 Why do future labours need to learn worldwide readiness skills

Future employers need employees own worldwide readiness skills, such as reading , writing and arithmatic. Why do employees need worldwide readiness skills? In the future, high economic growth countries need high wage positions, high opportunity jobs which need a large number of skills required of job candidates of these positions " job readinss" and not " job training" , which support developments of these importance and widely desired skills won't only support the success to high-opportunity positions, but also be developed for future success in the competitive global economy. Because real-time business intelligence is needed for the talent marketplace to employ talent employees. So, it explains that it will have many future employers hope to employ owning readiness skillful employees to help them to develop their businesse intelligently. Hence, present employees ought need to hard to train readiness skills to prepare whose future employers' job requirements in the future competitive global job market.

2.2 Why these occupations need readiness skills

In the future these occupations will need to raise readiness skills. For example, mathematical science, teachers (post-secondary), management analysts, computer and information systems, managers, first-line supervisors of construction traders, solar photovoltaic installers. All of these occupations , employers need staffs to own good readiness analytic ability to help them to do more accurate real-time business intelligent decisions. The representative occupations include oral and written communication skills, project management, teamwork, marketing and creativity . Moreover, they need to own specific technology skill, deep science and math or even most business skills as well as these skills are "soft" skills more than hard skills. These kinds of occupation employees need own cooperative effort, creativity, problem solving, detail orientation and integrity personal characteristics, which are relevant across all knowledge and domains.

Therefore, in the future, science, technology,engineering and mathematics relevant occupations need to own more readniness and analytic skills more than othe kinds of occupations. Because these organizations need those professionals on knowledge acquisition, literacy analysis, synthesis and critical thinking skills that will impact their organizations to bring more critical thinking beneficial team culture. These occupational top skills will include oral and written communication skills, project management skill, team oriented skill, marketing and creativity skills, problem solving skill, detail oriented skill, self-motivated skills, management and analytical skills, coaching skill, business process modeling skills, work independent skill, strong leadership skills, management experience and business requirements gathering. All of these skills which will be future employers who need to employ these kinds employees who own these skills in preference. Also, all of these skills concentrate on soft skills more than hard skills. It seems that when above occupational applicants who own any one of thes skills, evn more than one skills. Then, he/ she will have more chance to be selected to employ. Also occupation specific skills requirements are more needed to compare cross-functional skills for above of any one occupation. Because the high concentraton of cross-functional skills require " job readiness" and not " job training" for success, e.g. communicaton, integraton and presentation skills, entrepreneurialism and related skills, microsoft office software skills.

Of particular interest is communication, integration and presentation skills. These skills include ability to seek, evaluate and examine information and data create a reasoned position, present findings and make a case for or advocate for position. So, these skills are very important and they can help future applicants who expect to win any kinds of these positions easily. However, the hard skills can help these applicants to be more successful to win any kinds of these positions when they own these hard skills, e.g. microsoft offic, powerpoint, excel , word, microsoft project etc. softwares.

In conclusion, the global economy is dynamic and many of the skills required for positons in the future will need good technologies and work practices to be developed. The number of skills required t be successful in the jobs forecast to be most in demand in the future is growing. So, it explains that why future any one of these occupations which will need soft skills more than hard skills, due to organizations like to employ the employees who own managerial and analytical effort more than hard skills productive effort to assist their organizations to develop more easily.

2.3 Data -analysis skill needs

In the future, most organizations will have a number of jobs that include data analysis. Economists and labor market forecasters predict occupations need data analytical skill will need much. In addition, fast technological development means th types of technologies and applications workers in this field will need to be familiar with data analytical skill rapidly. It seems that data analytical jobs will have new job opportunity to employees with in-demand skills in future global labor market.

Why and how do employers demand for data analysis skills? Data analysis skills mean the ability to gather, analyze and draw practical conclusions from data as well as communicate data findings to others. The occupations include: data analyst, data scientist, statistician, market research analyst, financial analyst,research manager. In business career, many employers expect to employ statisticans, operations researh analysts, market research analysts and marketing specialists to assist their organizations to gather useful data from market in order to analyze and draw practical conclusions and finding the best solutions or methods to win their competitors.

Therefore, these data analysis jobs will have much need. Large size organizations with 500 or more employees were more likely than small or medium size organizations with 25 to 499 employees to plan hired data analysis positons in the future. For example, human source department will use big data to help make strategic decisions. How HR uses big data . HR will use big data for sourcing, recruitment, or selection, identifying causes of turnover and/or employee retention strategies or trends, managing talent and performance. Why organizations do not use big data. It is possible that they lack of knowledg expertise, the majority of organizatons will have data analysis positions within accounting and finance department, human resources department, business and administration department, information technology department, marketing, advertising and sales department, supply chain and operations department, research and development department, customer service department and other departments. So, future data analysis skill will need to used in different organizational departments.

However, publicly and privately owned for-profit organizations were more likely than government organizations to have data analysis positions in the marketing, advertising and sales function. Also, data analysis skills are required to different levels in any organizations , such as entry level, non-management / individual contributor level, mid-level management level, seniot management or executive level. The analyst, research analyst, market research analyst, scientist-based titles include: data scientists , research scientist, scientist, other descriptive titles include researcher, statistician, mathematician and other . So, data analysis positions will have many different skills to be selected to any one data analysis professional. For example, the data analysis professional can select either to learn the ability to interpret and communicate data analysis results skill or to learn how gathering or analyzing data skill. So, data analysis skill is not onlyone skill, it is more than one skill to let any one employee to select to learn.

Why do organizations need data analysis professionals? On workforce planning aspect, organizatons expect to let strategic direction and content of workforce needed for future business objectives easier, analyzing workforce: supply analysis, demand analsis and gap analysis more earier, developing action plan : recruiting and training plans to deal with gaps more easier, implementing action plan, monitoring, evaluating and revising plan more easier. So, organizations expect the data analysis professionsla can help them to solve these challenges, such as using of advanced technology solutons to integrate disparate planning sources; data availability and format; accessing to and understanding of the organization's data and analytics, developing business case to gain support from senior management and collaboration among HR staff, managers and executive easier. Future industries need data analysis professionals may include manufacturing health care and social assistance, scientific and technical service, finance and insurance, educational services , government agencies, retail trade, transportation and warehousing, construction, utilities, accomodation, and food services, waste management and remediation services, entetainment, and creation, real estate and rental and leasing , repair and maintenance, agriculture, forestry, fishing and hunting, personal and laundry services etc.

In conclusion, data analysis job need explains why future readiness and data analytical skills will be popular needed in globl labour market , due to these both skills are labour shortage and employers will need employees own big data readiness and data analytical both skills in order to win whose competitors more easier.

2.4 What are regional dynamic skills
of global labour market demand

Businessmen expect to improve better economic environment, they will prefer to recruit the most sought after skills of intelligent employees to bring positive beneficial impact to organizations. However, technology and digisation has had a significant influence on workers. Future globalization will trend digital economic development. Hence, it will influence workers' skills to be changed also. In fact, not all changes are positive because some workers will possible lose jobs, either due to new technology replaces their jobs or they lack enough effort to improve their skills in global digital economic labour market environment.

It brings this question: What are regional dynamic skills need whn digital busines environment is growing. In fact, organizations will continue to deal with skills shortages, labour markets across the global are continually changing. so, more employers and workers will need to adopt innovate working pattern, e.g. on call jobs, freelance jobs will grow popularly. The greater flexibility afforded to employ regardly.

Finally, digitalisation includes artificial intelligence, big data , online platforms. All these new technology will influence future employees how to worker. For example, they can apply online platform to work at home conveniently. So, they do not need to go to offices. They can finish their jobs and send to their employers by email easily. This kinds of job pattern can raise efficiencies and employers do not need go to offices often.

An important implication of innovating working which needs the employees who own digital skills in order to serve organizations more efficiently. So, employers are increasingly able to access demographics that were hitherto less active in labour markets. For example, future more women are joining the labour market because part time and self employment opportunities make it easier. This kinds of job pattern can raise efficiencies and employees do not need go to offices often.

An important implication of innovating working which needs the employees who own digital skills in order to serve organizations more efficiently. So, employers are increasingly able to access demographic that were hitherto less active in labour markets. For example, future more women are joining the labour market because part time and self employment opportunities make it easier to manage family with work life. So, digital skilling needs will cause many women lose jobs in possible. If the women lack digital job skills. Because high digital skill occupations need, like those requiring research, medical treatment and architectural design occupational digital skills are more common in the services sector, more women who own digital skill who can compete to win.

High digital skill occupations more easier than men because employers usually select female to do high skill occupations easier than make. However, if those professional service female employees can not learn how to apply digital skills to do these researchs medical treatmentm architectural design professional service jobs. Then, it is also different for these professional service femal employees to raise competition in global labour professional service market. So, these professional service female employees need to learn how to apply digital to do themselves jobs in future global professional service labour market. Otherwise, if the male professional service employees can attempt to learn how to apply digital skill to do themselves jobs in order to improve efficiencies and service performance to satisfy patients, such as medical service needs, school search service needs, construction firms' building needs. Then, the owning high digital technology skillful female employees will be more easier to find the professional service jobs which need digital skill more easier than the lacking digital skill female service professionals in future global digital service professional labour market.

On the other robotic communication skill need aspect, future employers expect workers to know how to communicate with robots to work efficiently in any working environment if the employers need robotc to serve their organizations. For example, communication between the robots on factory floors, and between people and robots could allow robots to start and stopr processes based on real-time conditions around them and alert people when there is a problem, so robots could increase their own efficiency if the workers could monitor themselves and determine when they needed maintenance; efficiency would also be improved if machines and robots could make production decisions on their own by. For example, ordering new suppliers when existing inputs into a production process run low. The increase in productivity of industrial robots will likely reduce the number of manual jobs on the shop floor.

At the same time, the increased output made possible by such robots will mean that manufacturers need more people in accounting, finance, sales, advertising and other roles. The increase in putput may also drive increased employment on manufacturers' supply chains. Hence, future employers expect to employ the workers who can know how to communicate with robots to work efficiently in order to raise productivity in any working environment. It means that it the worker can know how to control and communicate with the robots to work together in the team. Then, his/her communication and controlling robotic skill will help the organization's team to work efficiently and raise productivity in order to reduce time waste and human waste and resource waste considerately. So, future shortage of communication and controlling robotic skillful workers number will increase. It has much beneficial to workers who choose to attempt to learn how to communicate and control robots to work together in any working environment team efficiently. Because future employers will like to use robots to assist manual workers to attempt to raise productive efficiency in any working environment.

So, the need of employees who know how to cooperate or communicate with robots whose talent skills will be useful to any future employers.

Future global business leaders will need human machine cooperation skill. This technological skill includes artificial intelligence (AI and internet of things (IOT), will reshape our working change. These machines will participate to our daily working environment. For instance, many business leaders agree that automated systems will free-up their time as well as they also believe they'll have more job satisfaction by offloading the tasks that they don't want to do to intelligent machines.

Therefore, future leaders will expect humans and machines can work as integrated teams within their organizaton in order to their workforce and machines are already successfully working this way. So, they need to expect future employees can know or learn how to work with automated systems more easily, because many jobs will be participated by automated systems, e..g simple accounting tasks, legal administration tasks etc. clerical tasks. They will be participated with (AI) technology, it learns how to cooperate with (AI) technology to finish simplt clerical tasks efficiently.

Future workers will need have autrmated system operational skills: They include that how to operate automated systems to free -up workers' time. Workers will need to learn how to operate automated system to better with healthcare tracking devices workers will need to learn how to operate automated systems to absord and manage information in completely different ways. Workers will need to learn how to operate automated systems of smart machines to work as admin. in any orking environments. Workers need be needed to learn how to operate (AI) automated machines to mak more accurate clerical tasks or efficiencies. So, the automated system (robotic) operational skillful workers' demand and number will increase.

In the future, employers need automated machine manufacturing and service with workers cooperation reasons include that clear protocols, will need to be established if autonomous machines fail. So, they need their workers to learn how to control and manage and communicate with autonomous machines skillfully. They believe move they depend upon technology, the more they'll have to lose in the event of a cyber attack. So, skillful workers are real required to let them to know how to cooperate with autonomous machines more efficiently and easily. Computers will need to be able to decipher between good and bad commands, so future employers have much chance to need the owning automated machines operating workers to assist any robots to make more accurate good or bad decision when robots and workers have need to make immediate judgement in their any related job responsibilites aspect.

Therefore, future owning automated machines operating workers' skillful level will be high. It bases on automated machine manufacturing environment trend factor. Finally, future technology will connect the right employee to the high task at the right time. It implies that when future global employers began to accept to apply robots to help them to raise any productivities efficiently. It will influence many manufacturing positions which need to employ any proficient skillful workers who own automated machines operational skills to know how to communicate or manage or control , even supervise any robots to work in teams in any organizational manufacturing environment efficiently.

In the future, employers also expect employees to own sufficient digital vision and strategic skills, manifest among other things. They can know how to apply data to demonstrate any senior support and sponsorship digital technological skill. They expect to reduce a skill gap and avoid a lack of employee buying and a workforce culture to change in their digital technologicl manufacturing organizations. Future employers also believe outdated technology that can't work fast enough, data overload, privary and security concerns. So, it explains why it is possible that future employers also need digital working environment and automated robots machines to attempt to achieve raising productive efficient aim.

Moreover, it also explains why digital transformation need will be raised. The reasons include: They feel digital technology can gain employees' buying in , making customer experience a boardroom concern, achieving fair compensation , training and goals and strategy achievement more easily, tasking senior leaders with digital working environment change putting policies and technology to support a fully remote, flexible workforce , empowering lines of team work more efficient, teaching all employees how to code/understanding how to adopt to work with automatic machines or rots in any team efficiently. So, automate machine can raise efficiency in manufacturing society.

In conclusion, in the future business society, employees need to be stronger human machine partnerships. So , future manufacturing or service industries will have digital technology and automated machine robotic technology to assist workers to work in any working environment efficiently. They expect digital technology and automated machine robotic technology anticipation to workers' daily jobs in order to bring positive impacting to the customer experience from business owners to decision makers in marketing, customer service, research and developmnt and finance etc. They also expect technological productivity can bring positive relationship between technology and workers emerging technologies' impact on business and the way workers and automated machine work together.

In the future whether in general organizations need what kinds of employees' skills, they expect employee individual own. It is one interesting question. The common skills that employees need to own in order to any duties to any organizational departments efficiently, e.g. human resource, marketing, administrative, logistic etc. different departments. For hospital, school, business, professional occupations etc. different organizations. Whether future school ought implement one system educational method to teach different common skills to students in order to let them to leave schools to jobs more easier.

Future employers need to create new technologies including automation and algorithms, in order to create new high quality jobs and improve the job quality and productivity of the existing work of human employees in any organizations, e.g. accounting department will need intelligence (AI) to assist account clerks to do simple repeating accounting job tasks in order to share their work load and raise performance efficiency or legal organizations will need (AI) to assist law clerks to do simple repeating legal draft or legal document revising job tasks . All future general clerical jobs will apply (AI) technological tools to assist human to job, it will produce a comprehensive platform for managing workforce change. Hence, human manual(employees) need to learn how to adopt (AI) job participation to assist them to do different kinds of simple clerical jobs in any organizational administrative departments . They , clerical employees or white color workers need to learn how manage or dominate (AI) tool to improve job performance to be better. However, (AI) administrative workforce change, it is not only one kind of job automation change role in any physical offices. It influences future administrative clerks need change a more flexible manner, utilizing remote staffing beyond physical offices and decentralization of operations organizational workforce change.

Instead of (AI) participation to administrative job aspect, (AI) will also participate to manufacturing industry environment aspect, a new human-machine manufacturing workforce change will exist to any factories, warehouses working environment. Scientists predict that in present an average of 71% of total task hours across the industries are performed by humans, compared a 29% by machines. In this average is expected to have shifted to 58% task hours performed by humans and 42% by machines. In fact, nowadays, in terms of total working hours, no work task was yet estimated to be predominantly performed by a machine or an algorithm (AI). But, this picture is predicted to have somewhat changed with machines and algorithms (AI) on average increasing their contribution to specific tasks by 57% . For example, in the future, 62% of organization's information and data processing and information search and transmission tasks will be performed by machines compared to 46% today.

Therefore, these high technological skillful job change will bring negative influence to some demotive-skillful or low skillful labors to be dismissed, if they can not upgrade or raise or reskillgul their skill level to improve their analytical thinking , technology design and programming skills to cooperate with (AI) tools to work efficiently together in any organizational manufacturing or offie work environment. Because it will have many employers apply (AI) automation tools to participate with blue -color or whiate -color workers' tasks in order to raise efficiencies or improve performance in any working environment. So, it is right time to young or mid age employees need to upskill and/or reskill their rihgt type of skills to prepare future technology risch work environment changeing needs.

Future technological advances will permit an increasing number of tasks traditionally performed by humans to become automated. It seems that , such automation focused primarily on routine tasks, e.g. clerical work, bookkeeping, basic paralegal work and reporting etc. However, with the advent of big data, artificial intelligence (AI), the internet of things and ever-increasing computing power , i.e. the digital revolutions, non-routine tasks are also increasingly likely to become automated. For example, the recent development in robotics and 3D printing allow firms in advanced economies to locate production closer to domestic markets in fully aumomated factories. As a result, the future strongest incentive to automate because of their relatively higher labour costs will be reduced, when production automated will bring the negative influence to dismiss some foolish or low produtive or low skill workers , the owning high automated productive skillful workers will replace the low productive skillful workers in any factories' manufacturing environments. So, technological progress participates to raise quantity of jobs will cause result in significant job losses to low skillful workers. Because future employers will need many high automated productive employees to help them to cooperate with (AI) automated machine to work together efficiently. For example, many proportion of occupations at high risk is greatest in Germany and lowest in Korea, these countries organizations will accept to spend technology investments and education of workers to prepare future automatability manufacturing development successfully.

However, future automatability manufacturing development will bring technological unemployment in possible, due to workers need to adjust to the challenge of automation by switching tasks. Thus, preventing technological unemployment, also technological change does not just destroy jobs, but also generates new roles through its effect on productivity and the demand for new technologies. For example, it has been estimated that, for each high tech-job created in the industries , such as computing equipment or electrical machinery, some 4.9 % additional jobs are created for lawyers, taxi, drivers and waites in the local economy (Moretti, 2011).

Therefore, automated will also influence service industries' job nature change, e.g. taxi drivers need to apply (AI) automated machines to assist them to drive their taxis. When the passenger tells the taxi driver where he/she wants to go. Then, the (AI automated machine will follow the GPS road direction map to be indicated how to drive the taxi to go to the destination automatically . So, future taxi driver is one assistance role to assist the (AI) automated driving tool to dominate the (AI) tool to drive the taxi to catch the passenger to arrive the destination safety in the short time in possible. For another example, future restaurant waiters will need (AI) automated machines's assistance to help them to deliver or dispatch any foods and soft drinks to send to the identified eater's table carefully in accurate and efficient service performance way from the kitchen, in especially in the busy time and many people are sitting in the large size restaurant environment. So, future, waiter roles will be the leader , they need to manage or control or supervise the (AI) robotics how to make decisions to arrange to dispatch which foods or soft drinks to the different tables in preference immediately. Also, future law clerks need to supervise or manage the law robotics how to help them to make decisions to do revision or draft or filing legal tasks in preference in order to avoid any typing words are mistaken to type on computers or revised draft in wrong way to assist manual legal clerks' mistaken words are appearanced on any legal documents. So, the law clerk future role will be the trainer role , he/she eeds to teacher the robots how to check any words, e.g. grammers to correct them to be right grammers, or giving the accurate revision legal documents' instruction to let the legal robots to know how to revise each legal draft to prove whether which part of the legal draft will have wrong to be needed to revise.

In conclusion, future many manual workers' service or manfacturing job natures will become automated assistance to robotics. So, employees need to upgrade their skills in order to adopt new technological work nature change.

Reference

Moretti, E. (2011) local labor market in O, Ashentelter and D. Card (eds.) handbook of labor economics, Elsevier, North Halland.

Becoming talent human how influences social changes

Nowadays we tend to think about social and digital technology more from a personal or consumer perspective than their business or professional applications, but as the Digital Era continues to progress, many of technology's most profound impacts are likely to be in the world of work. In addition to changes in product and business development, knowledge management, data analysis, and other operational processes, transforming talent management will be a key priority for organizations striving to be employers of choice.

● Digital technology encourages to create talent human

Why does digitial technology encourage to create talent human or excite human to learn new things ? The human capital implications of social and digital technologies impact virtually everyone, regardless of the type of organization they work for, their profession, their functional area, or their career stage. That means that the talent management functions in all organizations, as well as the professionals who staff and lead them, have a critical role to play in ensuring the efficient and effective transition and transformation from Industrial Era models and processes to their Digital Era upgrades.

It's no surprise that talent management has already become more "high tech." Many employment related activities have been digitized, and there has been a corresponding increase in employee self-service. It's important to remember, however, that digitization is not the same thing as digital engagement, and that the rise of "high tech" solutions doesn't necessitate the loss of a "high touch" approach to managing an organization's human assets. Transforming talent management requires digitization, to be sure, but it also involves leveraging social and digital technologies in ways that promote and enhance communication, collaboration, and engagement - not just between an employee and the organization, but between and among employees themselves.

Talent Acquisition

The logical place to start when talking about the impact of social and digital technologies on talent management is talent acquisition, where the greatest advances have been made. Anyone who has searched and applied for jobs in the past 10 years is very familiar with how technology has transformed the application process, which in most organizations (and virtually all large ones) is now almost completely digitized and automated. However, there are other ways in which social and digital technologies are impacting talent acquisition that may not be as well-known or commonly understood. Social media sites in particular (such as Facebook, YouTube, and Pinterest) are a great way to promote an employer's brand and offer realistic previews of work life, people and culture in organizations. Online games and simulations can also be used to get a sense of what working for an organization would be like, and give organizations themselves an opportunity to determine if a prospective candidate would be a good cultural fit and potentially successful.

On organizational working environment aspect, some employers are recognizing the value of digital alumni networks or communities to maintain strong relationships with former employees. One of the primary motivations for doing this is that the employees may return one day and/or make referrals to or from their personal and professional networks. Similarly, talent networks enable organizations to establish and maintain relationships with professionals in key areas like IT and engineering, even when there isn't a current opportunity to have those folks be a part of the organization. Moreover, social media can bring positive influence to impact organizations to encourge employees to attempt or feel needs to learning new things for their tasks needs. Due to social media has actually transformed every stage of the recruiting process in significant ways - so much so that the traditional recruiting funnel can be recast in "social" terms. At the top of the funnel are activities like social advertising (i.e., placing job ads on social networks like Facebook), social sourcing (i.e., searching for candidates who meet certain criteria on networks like LinkedIn), and social referrals (i.e., having current employees share position openings with their online personal and professional networks). And at the bottom of the funnel is social screening (i.e., reviewing a candidate's public activity in social networks to identify potential hiring risks).

● Learning management is needed to feel needs to any organizations

Learning management is probably the another most advanced area when it comes to adopting and adapting to new technologies. As with recruiting and other processes, the initial advances are in the area of digitization, with social software applications evolving next. One of the obvious digital impacts is the increased use of elearning and online learning platforms with self-paced study. There are also countless instructional videos on the web, both free and fee-based, that address a virtually unlimited range of topics. And we can't forget MOOCs - massive, open, online courses - which have proliferated in the past couple of years. Finally, many organizations have also started to leverage tablets and other mobile devices for learning, as well as using simulations and games to help employees develop specific skills. In addition to offering training through a variety of multimedia channels, organizations are increasingly using a range of digital tools for assessing employees' skills. They're also allowing employees to play an enhanced role in identifying their key skill sets and training needs, and can even have them create their own learning and development plans. Allowing employees to take a more active role in their own learning and skills management enables organizations to develop and maintain a more complete and accurate knowledge and skills database, which in turn enables them to maximize the value of the workforce in which they've already invested.

1. Formal learning management systems and platforms are also beginning to incorporate social technologies in a variety of ways. Promoting connections and interactions among participants, as well as with the instructor, can enhance the learning experience both during and after a course. Creating course-based cohorts that allow people to continue to interact with each other via a digital

community - even when their shared learning experience is face-to-face - can promote both knowledge transfer and retention, in addition to increasing commitment and engagement through interpersonal connections.

2. Informal learning - which is now also referred to as social learning - is greatly enhanced by social technologies as well. In fact, this is probably the greatest opportunity and area of growth for organizations of all types and sizes. Through private social networks, intranets and other internal platforms that have incorporated social technology elements, organizations are better able to facilitate employee learning as they perform their job duties and complete work activities. Along with the networks themselves, features like advanced search, identified subject matter experts, digital communities of practice, wikis and more enable employees to access and learn from colleagues who are not just next door or down the hall, but even in another city, state or country!

As organizations move forward with leveraging technology to enhance learning initiatives, it will become increasingly important for them to address issues related to digital literacy and digital competencies. For the past several decades we've generally taken what I refer to as an LIY, or Learn It Yourself, approach to digital knowledge and skills. Although organizations may invest in teaching someone how to use a specific application related to their job, they make virtually no investment in helping individuals learn how to use general digital tools like Microsoft Office and even email. Left to their own devices, most people - and I include myself in this group- are much less efficient and effective at using these tools than they could or should be. As our tools get even more sophisticated, we need the foundational knowledge and skills to be able to use them well - and this foundation should probably be provided via more formal training. In other words, many people need to be "taught how to learn" in the Digital Era. If organizations aren't going to provide the formal training workers need to do that, it's probably in an individual's best interests to pursue those kinds of development opportunities on their own.

● What are social influences on human behavior when talent human number increases?

Social Influences on Human Behavior Because human beings are social and learn from observation rather than depending entirely on instinct, almost all aspects of human psychology and behavior are socially influenced. Languages, modes of dress, gender roles and avoided taboos are all agreed upon at a group level and form the basis of culture. What are the characteristics of social change? Small-scale and short-term changes are characteristic of human societies, because customs and norms change, new techniques and technologies are invented, environmental changes spur new adaptations, and conflicts result in redistributions of power. This universal human potential for social change has a biological basis.

This universal human potential for social change has a biological basis. It is rooted in the flexibility and adaptability of the human species—the near absence of biologically fixed action patterns (instincts) on the one hand and the enormous capacity for learning, symbolizing, and creating on the other hand. Because human beings are social and learn from observation rather than depending entirely on instinct, almost all aspects of human psychology and behavior are socially influenced. Languages, modes of dress, gender roles and avoided taboos are all agreed upon at a group level and form the basis of culture.

On conclusion, when one country can create many talent human, e.g. students, workers. Then they can bring more positive attribution to help or assist themselve country to develop rapidly. Consequently, the country's economic growth speed will be rapid. So, I believe that it has close relationship between economy growth and talent human number to any countries in nowadays societies.

IBM founder successful factor

When "IBM" Micro soft firm is building its computer business in US in the beginning. It must encounter much problems, e.g. introducing and persuading computer users to accept and feel what the IBM software products can bring advantages to them to compare other kinds of similar computer software or desktop products when they turn on their computers to use at homes or offices or libraries or anywhere. So, IBM must need to spend much time to let them to accept to use its software products and computers in computer market. Why do they must need to buy IBM micro soft to use? It is one influential question to need to solve their psychological problem.

IN the beginning, because it is a kind of new software product invention in the beginning. Desktop computer is not very popular to be used in global. So, it brings the competition is serious between IBM and Big Apple both computer brands. When Big Apple computer is the main competitor to threaten Micro Soft exists in this computer market. How can Bill Gates IBM founder attract many Big Apple computer users to choose to buy its any software and desktops to use in the beginning.. Because Big Apple brand was popular to be accepted to use its computers and software products by computer users in the beginning. So, Micro soft IBM must need to spend much time to let Big

Apple computer clients to accept to use its any software or desktop computers products when laptops did not been invented before 2000 yr. So, Big Apple is one monopoly computer firm in computer market in the 1980 year. I shall indicate these important factors to explain how IBM can develop its computer market in success as below:

Bill Gates , IBM founder is one computer university student, although he did not graduate, because he felt his software invention can bring high technology to help humans to apply computer " word" software to replace hand writing conveniently. So, any office administrative staffs won't need to spend long time to write any documents or apply typewriters to type. Hence, Micro soft, IBM " word" software invention can help office jobs raise efficiency and documents productivities as well as reduced staffs number in office because computer typing speed is rapid to compare handwriting or typing machines. Employers can pay less salary to employ less office workers when they had learnt how to apply " word" software to do any clerical tasks. So, it seems that Big Gates can tough computer users' hopeful needs in offices or homes. So, global offices start to apply computers and Micro soft " word" software to do their administrative tasks and students and teachers can apply this kind of clerical software to do their homework and teaching tasks in schools and homes or libraries. It seems customers number will increase and Micro soft, IBM can attract many Big Apple computer clients for long time.

Intellectual means that to students with exceptional abilities in one or more of the learning areas(i.e. English, the arts, health and physical education, learning languages, mathematics, and statics , science and technology). Creativity means to students with general creative abilities as evidences in their abilities to problem –find and problem –solve , and their innovative thinking and productivity as well as social or leadership means that students with interpersonal and intra-personal abilities and qualities, which enable them to act in leadership roles. However, these are not the important personal characteristics factors to influence Bill Gates personal success. I assume that he can not achieve his software and computer invention in success if he lacks hard working attitude and learning any new technological knowledge attitude, even he own talent, creative and leadership abilities because one successful scientist must need to spend long time research tasks and he also needs to pursue any new technological knowledge to help him to solve any research problems. Otherwise, he must forget his scientific research when he feel difficulties and disappointment when he encounters any problems in his researching process. Hence, I feel that hard working and pursuing learning is the important factors to influence Bill Gates success. In fact, Bill Gates individual success. It is not only his talent and creative factor. I believe his hard work attitude and learning any new technological knowledge mind factor is more important to compare his personal characteristics. His hard working behavior on computer software research aspect, it can bring more influential to his final invention in success more than his talent and creative natural ability. So, I feel his non-natural effort, such as his hardworking and learning new technological knowledge and research attitude is his important factor to influence his software invention and laptop and desktop invention in success.

How did Bill Gates grow up? His father is one lawyer. So, it proved that he can not learn any scientific knowledge from his father teaching, he has only technological teacher can teach him some computer science basic concept knowledge in school. Hence, Bill Gates family is not a scientific background family. He may own creative and talent abilities to bring his success. When he left his university. Then he attempts to find or discover any new computer knowledge when he does any computer scientific investigation at homes or lab. However, he must encountered any several scientific research fails before he achieved the Micro software " word" software invention and then different types of desktops, even nowadays, laptops , smart phones technological communication products invention royalties in global computer market. So, Bill Gates is not only one successful inventor, he is also one successful businessman. He can have good leadership ability to lead his whole different departments to work efficiently and improve the best sale service performance and the most satisfactory products productive qualities to let his clients to feel habitually. So, his hard working factor can influence his whole IBM success till today.

However, Bill Gates is as a diligent learner. His early age became a diligent learner. He read the Word Book. Encyclopedia series start to finish. His parents also encouraged his appetite for reading by paying for any book, he wanted. Knowledge can help or hinder creativity. One needs to know enough about a field to move forward into more creative ways of thinking. So, none any ones can control or threaten Bill to stop to learn any new knowledge easily. His unique charters can influence his success, such as he is not limited to a willingness to overcome obstacles, willingness to take risks , willingness to tolerate ambiguity and self-efficacy. For example, he left his university to learn computer science, his reason ensures not due to his lazy or feeling failure to graduate. I ensure that he feel he has responsibility to invent one kind of computer software to attribute global office or home computer users to use and to let them feel this kind of software can raise office efficiency and productivity and it can bring rapid typing speed to let students or white color workers to finish their home work or office tasks in short time. The important factor is his confidence , he believed that he is the only inventor to invent this kind of unique software to attribute to any computer users to use in success. In fact, his confidence can help him to achieve his dream and earn much money and successful feeling and social high class position in our societies.

He also own unique personal characteristics, such as he have confidence to change accustomed or conventional thinking to unconventional thinking to bring human's new hope when one day any computer users buy his software or desktops or laptops to use. So, in the right place , at the right time with the right set of skill, all of these natural environment advantages can help him to create invention success. In the 1980 year, computer industry is needed to research any creative software products or desktops products from any one inventor.

By the late 1970s, the computing giant IBM had plans for marketing a personal computer for home use. They approached Microsoft to develop the standard operating system for their home computer models. Gates and Allen then went out and purchased for $50,000 an operating system called Q-Dos, which had been developed by Seattle Computer. Q-Dos Was compatible with the Intel processor that IBM intended to use. The two then adapted Q-Dos system and presented it to IBM. Money magazine quoted Gates as recalling. (July 1986).

It can give one good business environment to help Bill to

build his computer software and computer products sale business in success at the moment. So, it is one right time to let Bill have chance to be one computer software and desktop inventor, and US is the only one country to provide any scientific resource to let him, Bill, American to research as well as there is lack any computer scientists at the time. So, the right time and right place and right skill environments can help Bill to be one successful inventor. All of these factors are external environment factors to assist him to carry on his computer scientific research tasks in success. If he born in one developing country, such as India or China. I believe that he can not be one successful inventor in possible because these both countries can not provide good technological resources to support him to carry on his computer science research at the moment. So, external environment factor will influence him to be one successful inventor in success in the past.

Conclusion, IBM success is due to the founder, Bill Gates whose hard work and acceptable to attempt to learn any new technological knowledge personal attitude more than creative, talent factors. Moreover, the right time, right place and right skillful external environment factors can assist or help him to become the first technological inventor easily. If he born in one low technological resources and skills supplying country, his country lacks enough money and computer technological professor to teach his computer basic knowledge and research expenses. I believe that his invention will have encounter fail in possible. So, external resource supplying environment factor as well as his personal abilities and invention attitude factor will influence his final invention in success.

Amazon ecommerce founder successful factors

Nowadays, we are encountering digital age period. Many customers choose to apply websites and mobile apps to buy their products. So,many merchants also choose online e-commerce channel to build online purchase platform to raise its competitive ability in online e-commerce market. So, customers can apply mobile apps or merchants themselves websites to buy any products in any time and any places conveniently.

However, in electronic (ecommerce) industry, Amazon is the global largest online retail delivery provider. It sells different kinds of products from internet, e.g. books, electronic products, music, movie Cd, DVD, magazine, garden and homw useful tools, children toys, computer, software, even, cars from online channel to global online shoppers. So, there ate many online buyers choose to buy any products from Amazon web services middle channel. In fact, its products prices can be low, a wide selection, ease website use and convenience to meet all of its customers' needs in one virtual store. So, it can still own the high share market in online retail delivery service industry. I shall indicate that Amazon successful factors as below:

It has a clear aim or mission. It's mission is to be Earth's most customer-centric company , where people can find and discover anything , they want to buy online. So, it will gather data ro analyze whether why and how customers will select to buy the kinds of products from internet. Why do its customers forget to choose to buy any products from shops and they choose Amazon to buy their preferable products from online? I believe that it has these characteristics to attract them such as:

It can provide return after sale services within the reasonable time when the customer feels that he does not need to use the product or feels unsatisfactory to the product, then he can return the product to Amazon and Amazon must refund money to him as well as it can provide free charge of grocery delivery service to every customer home. Instead of these attractive service, it also began to enter publishing market. In July 2002, Amazon started offering services to website developers, marketings its kindle

product, aimed at capturing the publishing market for digital books, then it can sell paper books from online channel. It aims to let readers can choose to either download to read ebooks from its website or borrow ebooks to read from its electronic library or paid visa to print paper books to deliver their paper books to their homes conveniently. So, readers feel that they can enter Amazon publish website to choose any interesting books to buy or borrow to read , they do not need to go to book stores or libraries.It is Amazon's competitive and attractive and unique strengths to build its customers on this online retail market.

On its organization mamagement aspect, it has one effective and efficient management strategy. It has a good CEO manages his e-commerce business. Bezos has been chairman of the board of Amazon , since he founded the compnay in 1994. Amazon has a limitless stock on hand at all time, it enables Amazon to collect high margins when providing low prices, and lets customers to feel consideration every second. So, when the customers feel any enquiries, his customer service team members can apply its intra website email message channel to send email to answer his enquiries when they enter Amazon intra-website email message channel to send email to ask them any enquiries and they can reponse their enquiries immediately in any time or they can phone to Amazon customer service hotline to enquiry them directly. So, its customer service staffs can answer their enquiries either by phone or email communication in short time rapidly. They won't delay to response their enquiries to avoid they feel worry or unhappy or complain. So, efficient customer service performance can help it to satisy its customer service needs and build good customer service relationship and repeat purchase chance will increase also.

However, global online retail marketplace is expanding rapidly. So, Amazon will have many new or potential online retail competitors, if it neglected to improve its strategy to adapt every online customer individual need or purchase taste, due to customers' purchase need will often change, such as price demand, product delivery time demand, customer service demand etc. spects. So, Amazon needs have different market strategies in different time in order to attract customers' choices in different economic environment, if it hoped to keep online retail leader position.

For example, how to encourage or raise customers' online purchase desires when economy is poor environment. When many people loss jobs, due to many businesses liquidate and loss many clients. So, they need to dismiss many staffs. Then, in society, many families will reduce their consumption desires because their parents loss jobs. So, Amazon needs improve its strategies on above different aspects in order to attract or persuade them to spend much time on internet shopping activities.

Instead of organization management aspect and customer service aspect, the other critical success factors for developing an e-business strategy to Amazon, they may include: How to apply network technology to keep long term close relationship between Amazon its e-commerce organization, online customers, partners, stakeholders and product suppliers. It is very important to influence Amazon's success, because Amazon , such as the e-business delivery service provider will loss the kinds of product sale chance, if the product providers dislike its sale delivery service or feel satisfactory to

its sale strategy or promotion methods or when its online sale delivery service can not let its customers feel its online sale delivery to be satisfactory. Hence, online sale delivery service performance is very important to influence Amazon's success.

Moreover, in its business model, Amazon.com also needs have these key succes factors. They may include: Building strong brand name location, because when online shoppers can remember its brand or loyalty easily when it is famous. Then they won't choose any online retail delivery providers to replace its delivery service easily. So, building one famous and confident online retail delivery service provider loyalty or brand , it can help Amazon to influence many online shoppers have confidence to choose its online retail delivery service in the first time. When they can often remember Amazon and feel it is only one online retail delivery serivce provider, the repeat online purchase chance will also increase, due to they only choose to click on its website to choose any kinds of products to buy more easily.

So, Amazon.com's marketing strategy is needed to design to strengthen the Amazon brand name, increases customer traffic to the Amazon.com web sites, builds customer loyalty, encourages repeat purchases or attracts them to clicks on its websites again to develop incremental products and retail delivery service revenue opportunities. Also, how to design its efficient products delivery value

to let product buyers to feel. This factor is important to influence Amazon's products delviery service in success in online
retail delivery service market. Moreover, Amazon publish service also needs to build attractive reading feeling to let readers to satisfy its reading provision needs to replace book stores or libraries.

On conclusion, Amazon ought need to continue to change its marketing strategies in order to adapt to its online retail product delivery service changes as well as lets they believe that it is one online customer care product delviery service provider to comapre other online retail delivery service providers, if it hopes to keep its online retail relviery provider top leader position in this e-commece market.

Successful president personal characteristics

Every country must have one president, he/she needs to manage his/her country to keep the crime ratio reduces to let its citizen feel to live safely and build good economic environment to let buisnessmen have any kinds of business chance to do their import and export business, provides enough education resource to let young people have chance to learn etc. different aspects social responsibilities. So, one successful president must also be one successful leader, he/she is such as one CEO , he/she needs to know how to organize his/her organization to achieve the most efficient and the most effective performance. It brings this question: What are the president personal characteristics, he/she must need to own in order to achieve above
any one responsibilites successfully. I shall indicate these similar personal characteristics to every president, he/she ough own as below:

What is a great leader or CEO or president their similar personal characteristics? What is a popular leader, president, CEO reasonable performance? Are they the either same or some difference? Are they the result of the same or different factors? I feel that their same personal characteristics have these similar characteristics, such as they can create

themselves own greatness, has long been challengedby scholars from diverse disciplines who analyze leadership appeal and performance into broad impersonal forces and social -structural factors. Such as president case, if he/she hopes that his/her citizen feels he/she has enough abilities to solve any social problems. He/she must have abilities to know or evaluate

whether which kind(s) of social problem(s), he/she must need to solve in order to avoid this social problem continues grow to cause more difficulties. For example, if the country has many young people feel housing supplying number is not enough or young people feel difficulty to find jobs to do. Then the president needs to find what the factors cause these both social problems to young people. It is due to many young people are low education level, but there are many employers need high education level workers more than the low education level workers. Then, the factor ought be due to their low education level causes they feel difficulty to find jobs in job market. Then, the president ought concentrate on providing more skillful education to let these young people to learn different kinds of skills, e.g. computer, building, accounting etc. skills in order to them to apply their skills to find any jobs more easily. They feel housing supplying number is shortage, the solutions may seek new lands, or refill sea to increase land on sea, or rebuilding the old building etc. different methods to increase more lands to build more houses. So, one successful president could analyze whether these two social problems , which one is more important and young people hope to solve in the short time as well as he/she ought attempt to find the effective solution(s) to solve these both social problems within one to three years.

Because long time solution, it will cause young people feel satisfactory and complaint government. Because one succcessful president needs have good analytical abilites to judge whether next steps , he she needs to do in order to achieve the best solution.

Can these phenomena of greatness and appeal among political leaders or president be analyzed in psychological terms? They ought have these personal characteristics as below:

Leader characteristics means that the leader's personal appeal and performancewhen structural and traditional factors are held constant.He is set apart from ordinaryof personality to posses a certain quality of personality from ordinary men and treated as owed with supermatural , superhuman, or least specifically exceptional powers or qualities. Because president's

responsibility is different to CEO. One CEO only needs to manage his firm, it concerns to solve any firm's internal strategic challenges.Otherwise one president needs to manage whole country. It concerns to solve any social problems. So, I believe that one president's responsiblity must have more than one CEO's responsibility. He needs to concern how to let citizen feels satisfactory to live in this country. Otherwise, they will feel satisfactory to complain their government, even they can perform anti-threat government behaviors, e.g. many Hong Kong, France, US,UK people are walking on the road, or young people damage any roads or shops facilities. Their behaviors can perform their unsatisfactory emotion to let HK government to know. So, one president must need to supervise his government departments, e.g. education, transport, house and building and land, police force, administrative, leisure, environment protection etc.

How they can implement the most effective strategies to let the country's citizen feel satisfactory to live in the country. It seems that the successful factor is that how to avoid young or old

citizen feels unsatisfactory to complain or do anti-social damage behaviors. If one country have one long time anti-social damage behaviors, then it will bring long time unsatisfactory feeling or negative emotions to itself citizen and they will feel that the president's performance is poor and even he/she needs to be dismissed in possible.

So, one successful president needs to know whether what the social suitation or what social needs to its citizen are. In fact, any country's young people must consider education, jobs, living needs as well as old people must consider retirement, leisure needs both aspects. So, these departments' responsibilities are ususally much to compare other departments in government organization , such as education, house and land and building, labor departments because these are every people's basic living needs. For example, living and jobs must be needed to eveyr young people. They must need money and house. Otherwise, old people do not want to work, they must need have good retirement welfare to compare young people when they are facing old age. So, one successful president needs have abilities to solve these social problems if he /she hopes that his/her country has many young and old people like him or her to be their president.

Every country needs one effective election to elect themselves president. So, one president needs have good influential ability to persuade his/her citizen to elect him/her in order to he/she can do this president position. During this election process, he/she must need have good leadership abilities to lead his/her election team to know how to use what
methods to advertise and build good image or loyalty to let his/her citizen believes and have confidence that he/she can do this president position to satisfy their any needs in society. So, how to lead his/her team in order to achieve the high vote number to support his/her president election, this leadership ability factor will influence him/her to be succeeded in the time of selection. If he/she can not lead his/her selection team how to persuade citizen to believe he/she has ability to manage their country, then he/she will have high chance to let many citizen to vote him/her and then he/she can not do this president position. So, the president election participant personal leadership ability will influence whether he/she can succeed to do this president position in the president election process. So, leadership ability is very important to cause anyone to be president in success in the
election process.

Successful fiction author personal characteristics

In publishing industry, there are many different kinds of topics to let authors to write. However, in author career, it has two both topics choices, either ficition or non-fiction. So, fiction authors must need have more creative mind to write any horror, science, sad, happy, fun etc. stories. Otherwise, non-fiction authors, e.g. teaching writers , they must not need more creative mind , because they only need to apply theories, e.g. economy, accounting, law, science, engineering etc. different subjects to support their conclusion

to write any teaching books. Mostly technical writing does have something to teach writers, particularly in the areas of organizational behaviors and research skills, it has little relationship to the ability to write a novel , such as creative mind ability. So, one fiction author must need have good creative mind to compare one non-fiction author. It is the personal characteristics between fiction and non-fiction author.

Every writer has his or her own experience, and every writer has his or her own ideas about writing, so what any one writer may think

can only go so far.But there are some basic principles that seem to hold in vast majority of cases to every fiction author, they have these same characteristics. However, to be one successful ficition author, he also needs have these personal characteristics, instead of creative ability as below:

In english novel, it must need have a theory, a conviction, a consciousness of itself to let readers themselves to make choice and comparison, because one attractive english novel must need have special theory to let readers to feel the author's creative mind to let readers to choose to read his/her story book more easily, before reader needs to spend time to choose which english novel to read.For exmaple, Hart Pover had about seven series. It can attract many readers to continue to read it. The reasons are due to this story author can touch readers' interesting to want to know that whether how the every story will continue happen in next step.So, when they read the serie one. They will hope this author continues to write the serie two in short time because they hope to know whether what will happen in this story step two. So, it explains that whether the story is attractive, it is the important factor to influence readers continue to read the author's story books. If the story is bore and it can not influence readers feel fun to know whether what the story will continue happen.

Then, it is difficult to influence the prior readers continue to pursue to read this next serie story. They will lose story pursuring desire

to continue to buy this author's next serie book to read. So, story content is very important to influence the readers' interest. If they

can feel the story is theory and fun and exciting when they read any stage in the story content of every chapter. Then, there are many

last serie readers , they will also feel reading need to read this story next serie, even more series. So, creative mind is very important

to influence the story author's success.

However, preparing a fiction to write, any fiction author needs follow these steps to prepare to write before. They may include:

Deciding on the idea(s) for your book, doing the research and creating an outline or structure for your book. Because one novel, you need

an ideastrong enough to carrythe reader through 300-400pages, and most ideas arenot that strong. You can combine more than one idea to produce multiple story-lines, and some authors have been very successful doing that, but the sum totalhas to be strong enough.How long would it take me to tell this story, and what kind of depth do I need from my characters to tell it?

I feel that one fiction author is similar to one non-fiction author, he needs to do the research. For example, one law or criminal author, he needs familiar these topics. If he has a background in the law or crimoinal investigation, or a particularfield of science. Then he can do less research tasks. Otherwise, when one fiction author plans to write one horror story. If he does not research any horror story authors' books to compare whether what their horror story contents are different and what the main contents which can attract or influence the readers to choose to read their books. So, he can compare some horror fictions whether what their attractive contents or

non-attractive contents are in order to avoid to create the non-attrative contents to let readers to read. So, researhing to read any last fictions , it will help the fiction author to avoid to write the bore contents to let readers to read in his new creative fiction.

The another obstacle to threaten any fiction author to be popular. It is how to discover the opinions between the living world and dream world to let readers to feel. It is one important factor to influence the fiction author's success. Because it is absolute that any fiction must be creative and dream. So, any readers will need to feel they are entering the dream world more than living world when they read any fiction or story. So, if the writer can give the living world actual opinions to let readers feel that it is possible to occur when they enter the dream world in their reading process. Then, it will bring exiciting feeling to let them to feel that this story seems to be occur in living world in possible. Hence, if the story' s content can let readers to feel it is not dream and it will occur in their living world in possible. Then, it will persuade them to continue to read again.

Successful scientistcs personal characteristics

Science job is exciting and fun and every scientist ought like this kind of job. Usually, scientists need to often research in lab. They

need to face unlimited fails in their research process and they also need to investigate and experiment, it aims to attempt to find any

not found discoveries to continue to carry on science research tasks. So, patience and continue researching and without fear failure attitude

must need to any one scientist. I shall indicate some similar characteristics to any one successful scientist as below:

Science training and experiment experiences are important factor to influence any one scientist's success , because any one scientist must need

to be taught to learn any kinds of science knowledge, such as space, earth, computer, biology, chemical, ocean, animal , engine etc. different kinds of science knowledge when they are university student. So, owning science training background must be one main factor to influence whether their science research can succeed. But, they can not also neglect the experiment experiences, because if they can have more times of experiment chances to let them to attempt to know whether why their every time experiment is possible failure. Then, they can improve their next experiment to avoid the errors occur again.

Learning and seeking or pursuring any new ideas that is also important to influence any one scientist's success. Because any new ideas will have chance to help them to solve the last or prior any problems. If they dislike to accept any new ideas or attempting to seek or discover any new ideas. Then, they will feel more difficulties to solve their any scientific problems and they can not achieve the researching success. So, learning and seeking or pursuring any new ideas attitude can help the scientist to increase scientific research succeess chance.

They need have scientifical moral or ethic responsibility. The moral issue will influence any scientist's success. For medical science example,

when one biological cell engineering scientist does not consider moral issue. He does the experiment to attempt to apply pig cell to put in human body.

He aims to pursue whether what change to the person when he owns pig cell in his body. Although, he argues that this experiment can help human

to discover any new medicine to fight any diseases. But, in fact, his experiment can bring negative moral behavior to cause the person to die in possible. So, the death risk is high, even legal system is accept that it is legal experiment in the country. So, one successful scientist ought own high level moral standard to carrying on any experiments in his science research career any time.

Learning to enjoy the process of writing and presenting. Because every scientist needs to write any research to let anyone to know. So, he

must need to enjoy writing and then present hie presentation to let anyone to know his successful research. One attractive presentation must need

good writing skill to let anyone to understand how and why the experiment can succeed and what the experiment can attribute to human to enjoy. It is

one enjoyable new to anyone. So, if the scientist feel bore to write and present his final research result when he believe that his scientifical research is successful. Then, his research can not persuade anyone to believe his attribution is worth in society.

Finally, any scientist needs have much confidence. Because one confident scientist can have much successful chance to carry on any experiments. So, his successful chance time will be shorten. Otherwise, one lacking confident scientist will need long time to achieve his experiment in success because he lacks confidence will influence his experiment performance and judgement brings more errors. Then , long time experiment can also increase.

Improvement social change

CHAPTER FOUR

Reducing global environmental pollution advantages

What are the advantages to reduce global environmental pollution to our future societies? If we do not continue to avoid to cause air and water pollution from manufacture or driving car etc. business or enjoyment activities, what negative influences what are caused to our future societies? I shall attempt to explain as below:

Firstly , I shall discuss whether reducing greenhouse gases benefits air quality how and why it can save human future lives. Air quality "co-benefits" result mainly from reductions in air pollutant emissions from the same sources that emit greenhouse gases. For example, replacing a coal-fired power plant with a renewable electricity source, such as wind power, reduces both air pollutant and greenhouse gas emissions. Nowadays, our world has been slow to adopt significant actions to address climate change, as it is a long-term and global problem. The benefits of reducing carbon dioxide today are felt in the future, and since they occur globally, countries may take little action and rely on others to lead. On the other hand, better air quality and improved health are realized rapidly and locally, providing government leaders with tangible benefits from their actions to reduce carbon dioxide. For example, reducing greenhouse gases pollution , it can bring health benefits of Air Pollution Reduction to influence global has more fresh air to let we can breathe, then we can avoid air pollution breath to cause our lung hurt, even death easily. Air pollution is a grave risk to human health that affects nearly everyone in the world and nearly every organ in the body. Fortunately, it is largely a preventable risk. Reducing pollution at its source can have a rapid and substantial impact on health. Within a few weeks, respiratory and irritation symptoms, such as shortness of breath, cough, phlegm, and sore throat, disappear; school absenteeism, clinic visits, hospitalizations, premature births, cardiovascular illness and death, and all-cause mortality decrease significantly. The interventions are cost-effective. Reducing factors causing air pollution and climate change have strong cobenefits. Although regions with high air pollution have the greatest potential for health benefits, health improvements continue to be associated with pollution decreases even below international standards. The large response to and short time needed for benefits of these interventions emphasize the urgency of improving global air quality and the importance of increasing efforts to reduce pollution at local levels.

● The consequences of water and air and water and chemical pollution

Air pollution may bring these effects. Diseases such as amoebiasis, typhoid and hookworm are caused by polluted drinking water.Water polluted by chemicals such as heavy metals, lead, pesticides and hydrocarbon can cause hormonal and reproductive.A polluted beach causes rashes, hepatitis, gastroenteritis, diarrhea, encephalitis, stomach aches and vomiting. Pollution or the introduction of different forms of waste materials in our environment has negative effects to the ecosystem we rely on. How does pollution affect the ecosystem? There are many kinds of pollution, but the ones that have the most impact to us are Air and Water pollution.Pollution or the introduction of different forms of waste materials in our environment has negative effects to the ecosystem we rely on. There are many kinds of pollution, but the ones that have the most impact to us are Air and Water pollution. How does pollution affect humans? Harmful gases and particles in the air come from a range of sources, including exhaust fumes from vehicles, smoke from burning coal or gas, and tobacco smoke. There are ways to limit the effects of air pollution on health, such as avoiding areas with heavy traffic. Thus, air pollutants cause less-direct health effects when they contribute to climate change. Heat waves, extreme weather, food supply disruptions, and other effects related to increased greenhouse gases can have negative impacts on human health.

There are many kinds of pollution, but the ones that have the most impact to us are Air, Water, and chemical pollution. How does pollution affect humans? In the following paragraphs, we will enumerate the consequences of releasing pollutants in the environment. We cause most of the pollution and we will suffer the consequences if we don't stop. We are already seeing its effects in the form of global warming, contaminated seafood, increased cases of lung diseases and more.

We release a variety of chemicals into the atmosphere when we burn the fossil fuels we use every day. We breathe air to live and what we breathe has a direct impact on our health. Over 100 million years of healthy life are lost every single year as a result of air pollution. On average, that's the same as 1 year and 8 months of healthy life lost for every single person on Earth.

Air pollution is the world's 4th most lethal killer

Air pollution is the cause of 8.9 million deaths globally every year. That means that every 4 seconds, someone somewhere on the planet dies from air pollution. The UN has called air pollution the world's worst environmental health risk. Air pollution is also the world's 4th most lethal killer (following malnutrition, unsafe sex, and the lack of safe, clean water and sanitation).

Air pollution from car exhaust affects human reproduction

If pregnant women are exposed to air pollution from car exhaust, it can alter the structure of the chromosomes in the fetus and increase the risks of cancer and various birth defects.

Air pollution and climate change closely linked

The main cause of air pollution as well as climate change (CO2-emissions) is the burning of fossil fuels (oil, coal, gas). A change to greener alternatives such as solar or wind power will therefore help both the climate and human health.

How air pollution influences human health

Breathing polluted air puts you at a higher risk for asthma and other respiratory diseases. When exposed to ground ozone for 6 to 7 hours, scientific evidence show that healthy people's lung function decreased and they suffered from respiratory inflammation.Air pollutants are mostly carcinogens and living in a polluted area can put people at risk of Cancer.

Coughing and wheezing are common symptoms observed on city folks.

Damages the immune system, endocrine and reproductive systems.

High levels of particle pollution have been associated with higher incidents of heart problems.The burning of fossil fuels and the release of carbon dioxide in the atmosphere are causing the Earth to become warmer. Read about the effects of Global Warming here.The toxic chemicals released into the air settle into plants and water sources. Animals eat the contaminated plants and drink the water. The poison then travels up the food chain – to us.

Water Pollution Effects

Just like the air we breathe, water is vital to our survival. We need clean water to drink, to irrigate our crops and the fish we eat live in the waters. We play in rivers, lakes and streams – we live near bodies of water. It's a precious resource that can easily be polluted and the contamination can be transferred to us and affect our health.

The consumer society is powered by water

Everything we buy, use, eat takes water to produce. Our total use of water through the stuff we buy is represented by "The water footprint". The global water footprint is 9 trillion tons per year or almost 300,000 tons per second.

The consumer society is getting more and more thirsty

Global demand for freshwater is projected to increase 55 % between 2000 and 2050. By 2050, it will reach a massive 5500 square kilometers or 5.5 trillion tons. The main sources for the rise in freshwater use are industry and manufacturing with an expected increase of 400 %. In addition, water demand from electricity-generation will increase 140 % and domestic use 130 %.

The pollution of groundwater resources is increasing

280 billion tons of groundwater is being polluted annually. In 2000, Earth's groundwater resources were being polluted twice as fast as in 1960. Water polluted by chemicals such as heavy metals, lead, pesticides and hydrocarbon can cause hormonal and reproductive problems, damage to the nervous system, liver and kidney damage and cancer – to name a few. Being exposed to mercury causes Parkinson's disease, Alzheimer's, heart disease and death. A polluted beach causes rashes, hepatitis, gastroenteritis, diarrhea, encephalitis, stomach aches and vomiting.Water pollution affects marine life which is one of our food sources. Remember the stories of contaminated shellfish and how those who ate them died?

Plastic pollution

Plastic wasn't invented until the late 1800s and the production of plastic didn't take off until around 1950. But then it really took off. The world has produced over 9 billion tons of plastic since around 1950. 6.3 billion tons (over two thirds!) of this plastic have ended up in the environment - including our oceans. By 2025, there will be a staggering 100 bags of plastic for each foot of coastline in the world! At this point, the ocean will contain around one ton of plastic for every three tons of fish. By 2050, there could be more plastic than fish (by weight) in the world's oceans. Just imagine. Diseases such as amoebiasis, typhoid and hookworm are caused by polluted drinking water.

We live in an ecosystem where the action of one has the potential to affect the many. This can be a good or a bad thing, depending on what the action is. Our mistakes has polluted the environment that we live in and we are waking up and owning to the fact. We are trying to reverse the damage. The good news is that every positive action counts.

The small effort you make towards a greener environment can start a healing ripple effect. We may still save what is left of our natural resources and make the world a better place to live in for our future generation.

Chemical pollution

Global production of synthetic chemicals is around 250 billion tons a year. Many of these chemicals find their way into our bodies and the consequences are horrifying. In samples from human beings, a study found as many as 420 different chemicals known to or suspected of causing cancer.Another study found an average of 200 industrial chemicals present in the cord blood of newborn babies.

287 different chemicals were identified in the cord blood.

180 can cause cancer
217 are toxic to the brain and nervous system
208 can cause birth defects or abnormal development.

This is truly terrifying. Especially since the global production of synthetic chemicals is expected to increase six-fold between 2000 and 2050.
On average, we already have around 700 synthetic chemicals in our body that are not a natural part of the human body chemistry. And we know very little about how the combination of these chemicals will affect us.

● Reducing air and water and plastic and chemical pollution different policies implement will be needed to different countries in our future societies.

Over the last decades, energy and pollution control policies combined with structural changes in the economy decoupled emission trends from economic growth, increasingly also in the developing world. It is found that effective implementation of the presently decided national pollution control regulations should allow further economic growth without major deterioration of ambient air quality, but will not be enough to reduce pollution levels in many world regions. A combination of ambitious policies focusing on pollution controls, energy and climate, agricultural production systems and addressing human consumption habits could drastically improve air quality throughout the world. By 2040, mean population exposure to PM2.5 from anthropogenic sources could be reduced by about 75% relative to 2015 and brought well below the WHO guideline in large areas of the world. While the implementation of the proposed technical measures is likely to be technically feasible in the future, the transformative changes of current practices will require strong political will, supported by a full appreciation of the multiple benefits. Improved air quality would avoid a large share of the current 3–9 million cases of premature deaths annually. At the same time, the measures that deliver clean air would also significantly reduce emissions of greenhouse gases and contribute to multiple UN sustainable development goals.

Given the dynamics of these factors and their complex interplay, what could be expected for future air quality around the world, and which determinants will be dominating? To answer this question, this paper identifies key factors that contributed to historic air pollution trends in different world regions, outlines conceivable ranges of their future development and examines their interplay on global air quality in the next decades. In particular, the paper provides a fresh perspective on how ambitious policy interventions could achieve clean air worldwide.

● Future projections of air pollutant emissions

A range of studies in the scientific literature explored the implications of these findings on future emissions and air quality. For a long time, future global air pollutant trends were mainly modelled in the context of long-term greenhouse gas emission scenarios . The early global studies on air pollutant emissions, notably the scenarios developed for the 'Special Report on Emissions Scenarios' and the 'Representative Concentration Pathways' that have been prepared for the Intergovernmental Panel on Climate Change (IPCC) proposed declining trends of (energy-related) air pollutants, due to autonomous technological progress and assumed pollution control policies along the environmental Kuznets hypothesis. Later, the improved understanding of the importance of targeted air quality policy interventions motivated a more differentiated approach to projections of air pollutant emissions, resulting in a wider range of air pollutant trajectories than in previous global scenarios. At the same time, the climate community addressed the interactions between decarbonization strategies and air pollutant emissions, both with the interest to reveal health benefits from low carbon policies and to explore the combined impacts of long-lived greenhouse gases and short-lived air pollutants (e.g. SO2 and black carbon) on radiative forcing and temperature increase . In general, the literature reveals strong impacts of ambitious decarbonization strategies on energy-related air pollutants SO2, NOx and PM, due to the phase-out of fossil fuels and the containment of all flue gases connected with carbon capture and storage. However, enhanced use of biomass as a greenhouse gas policy measure may lead to higher PM emissions . Compared to the climate-focused analyses that deal mainly with energy-related emissions and the role of climate policy interventions, only a few studies addressed the longer-term prospects for air pollution from a health- and ecosystems perspective. These studies take full account of other sources that also contribute substantially to population exposure to harmful air pollution, such as agricultural activities, waste management and materials handling. Also, they developed a more holistic approach towards the understanding of future trends in nitrogen emissions and their health and environmental impacts.

● How air pollution may influence the course of pandemics

The COVID-19 pandemic is causing devastating mortality, with the highest rates of intensive care unit hospitalization and morbidity among older adults, men, and those with certain preexisting conditions, most notably cardiopulmonary diseases, obesity, and diabetes. In addition, a host of interrelated socioeconomic factors—including race, ethnicity, occupation, and poverty—increase the risks of COVID-19 infection for people of color, health care professionals, and other essential workers. These factors are, in turn, influenced by conditions of the human environment including chronic levels of air pollution, most notably fine particulate matter (PM2.5) that is a well-established risk factor for death from cardiovascular and pulmonary obstructive diseases. This raises the question of whether long-term exposure to higher levels of PM2.5 increases the severity of COVID-19 and, if so, what measures might be taken to ameliorate those risks. This is the challenge addressed by Wu et al. in a new contribution to a developing series of papers for Science Advances that is dedicated to the study of pandemics from an environmental perspective.The ideal way to address questions about how PM2.5 pollution might influence the course of the pandemic would involve the study of detailed health datasets for very large numbers of people from all walks of life and locations. In this way, the potential effects of PM2.5 pollution might be evaluated in the context of other details about each individual's life history and conditions. The amount of time required for rigorous, extensive studies, however, conflicts with the swift nature of the COVID-19 pandemic. Addressing the potential impact of air pollution on COVID-19 mortality requires a more nimble approach to environmental policy decision-making.

COVID-19–related death counts (compiled by Johns Hopkins University for more than 3000 U.S. counties) and well-established PM2.5 pollution levels for each county. The results show that higher values of exposure to PM2.5 are positively correlated with higher county-level mortality after taking into account over 20 potentially confounding factors. Most notably, they conclude that an increase of just 1 µg/m3 in the long-term average of pollution is associated with a significant 11% increase in a county's rate of mortality.There are strong policy implications for these results. COVID-19, zoonotic influenza, and other potentially severe emerging zoonotic diseases are and will remain long-term threats to our species. Rapidly emerging datasets suggest that these threats are likely to be exacerbated by air pollution, even at the levels currently attained in the United States despite conscientious efforts to improve air quality. While incomplete and not yet fully vetted by the broader scientific community, pathfinding studies such as that of Wu et al. set the stage for more traditional environmental epidemiology research.

● Benefits of Reducing and Reusing policy

Recucing and reusing policy may help our earth to avoid serious pollution influences , such as prevents pollution caused by reducing the need to harvest new raw materials, saves energy, reduces greenhouse gas emissions that contribute to global climate change, helps sustain the environment for future generations, reduces the amount of waste that will need to be recycled or sent to landfills and incinerators and allows products to be used to their fullest extent.

● Ideas on How to Reduce and Reuse to implement

Buy used. You can find everything from clothes to building materials at specialized reuse centers and consignment shops. Often, used items are less expensive and just as good as new. Look for products that use less packaging. When manufacturers make their products with less packaging, they use less raw material. This reduces waste and costs. These extra savings can be passed along to the consumer. Buying in bulk, for example, can reduce packaging and save money. Buy reusable over disposable items. Look for items that can be reused; the little things can add up. For example, you can bring your own silverware and cup to work, rather than using disposable items. Maintain and repair products, like clothing, tires and appliances, so that they won't have to be thrown out and replaced as frequently. Borrow, rent or share items that are used infrequently, like party decorations, tools or furniture.

Thus, we are living in our earth. We are everyone has responsibilities to do environmental protection activities in every day, such as reduce and reuse activity will be our right environmental protection daily behavior, walking replaces to reducing to driving when we need short time to arrive the destination in any time, manufacturers need to buy air and water clean machines to avoid serious air and water pollution in their factory manufacturing processes, we need to reduce the frequeny to travel, e.g. one to two times travelling by air planes every year, then sky will have much fresh air in our earth, also airlines need to shorten flying time , e.g. New Zealand airlines only fly to Australia near distance country , it can not fly to US, or UK far away distance countries, China airlines only fly to Singapore, Japan etc. near distance Asia countries, they do not fly to US, UK far away disrance countries. Then, our future environment pollution will be reduced as well as we can have much fresh air to breathe and drive clean water to proplong our lives when we have health.

CHAPTER FIVE

Improving internet technology development

Why do we improve to improve internet technology? What long term social benefits will benefits if scientists can improve internet speed and reseach any information function ? I shall research these questions to give suggestion as below:

Why does internet improvement make life better? Internet of Things Benefits In short, the scale of change that IoT technology offers can be scary. At the same time, the benefits of a well-executed IoT strategy can be more need for an organization: Safety, Comfort, Efficiency. Also, the Internet offers teens the ability to make friends with peers with whom they would not otherwise connect. With pop culture deteriorating into many distinct subcultures, teens' interests are more variable than they have ever been.With internet communication, employees can effortlessly communicate with one another at anytime from anywhere in the world. This allows employees situated in different parts of the world to give their opinion and voice their concerns. Through internet access, individuals in developing countries are able to gain access to more of the modern economy. With internet connectivity, those living in remote areas can now easily take out microloans, participate in e-banking and more. A large share of respondents predict enormous potential for improved quality of life over the next 50 years for most individuals thanks to internet connectivity, although many said the benefits of a wired world are not likely to be evenly distributed.

● How internet can excite young to learn?

Internet can learn youngs to learn much different new knowlege when they research any questions and find answers from internet channel.

As one major aspect of teen life is social environment, changes in how teens connect impact the ways in which teens develop social skills. ** Luckily, the Internet offers many social-skill enhancement opportunities for teens of all different personalities . One advantage the Internet brings that the standard school environment cannot is the ability for teens to adjust their amount of social interaction. Teens who are extremely outgoing can spend their free time in social environments both offline and online, making new connections and catching up with friends.For example, a teen who finds large amounts of face-to-face interaction to be intimidating can use the Internet to engage in conversations while reducing the potential for social anxiety. In a way, this trains less social teens to be more social . In the past, these types of teens did not have the advantage of this social training provided by the Internet.

● Internet can encourage Social Network Growth

The Internet offers teens the ability to make friends with peers with whom they would not otherwise connect. With pop culture deteriorating into many distinct subcultures, teens' interests are more variable than they have ever been. Whereas in the past, children at school might have discussed the current top 40 when discussing music, today's kids define their musical tastes as specific genres, such as post-industrial, dubstep or jpop. Today, it's harder for teens to find peers who share the same interests in their schools. But online, not so. The Internet's social networks help teens find communities of peers who share similar interests, allowing a teen to grow his social network in a way that is specific to him 2. Today's teens are increasingly willing to make friends with different groups of people due to the ability to actually meet them, and this can be useful when they reach adulthood, a time in which accepting people of different backgrounds and demographics is crucial to career and academic growth. The Internet offers teens the ability to make friends with peers with whom they would not otherwise connect.

Today's teens are increasingly willing to make friends with different groups of people due to the ability to actually meet them, and this can be useful when they reach adulthood, a time in which accepting people of different backgrounds and demographics is crucial to career and academic growth.But the Internet can help teens foster self identity through exposure to new people, communities, hobbies and concepts. As teens go through more experiences, they learn more about themselves. And as the Internet can offer teens a wealth of experience, it can play the role of hastening the development of self identity.For many teens, the hardest part of life is figuring out identity.But the Internet can help teens foster self identity through exposure to new people, communities, hobbies and concepts.

● What Are Main Benefits of Internet Communication speed improvement ?

It may include as below:

1 Makes communication easier

Doing business through phone or mail doesn't work well ? Before the internet came into existence, the only way to communicate was through a phone. Or if you needed to send a note you had to send letters via mail. With the arrival of the Internet, staff and team managers can connect instantaneously without leaving their work place. ezTalks Meetings, a one-stop internet communication provider, is a perfect example. With this platform, participants can communicate as if they were right next to one another thanks to its quality video and audio. The tool comes with a rich set of features like screen sharing, cross platform chat, innovative whiteboard, and more.

2 Enhances collaboration

Internet communication brings teams together across the globe. Staff can collaborate easily without limitations and make more informed decisions instantaneously. This leads to reduced project timelines, cutting back on the time required to launch a new product/service. This piece of technology is also useful in education. Not only can students collaborate with foreign students, they can share ideas and learn about the diverse cultures out there. Parents can also become actively involved in their kids education by linking their children school with libraries, homes, and more. Millions of schools around the world are already using this technology to enhance learning.

3 It is cost effective

The cost of internet communication is significantly low when compared with other means of communication like face to face meetings and mail delivery. The technology connects you to your partners, colleagues, clients and suppliers from just about any location for a fraction of the cost required to host a one-on-one meeting. And as technology continues to become more efficient, the cost of online communication continues to drop significantly. With the traditional face to face meeting, you need to spare time, cash to travel and so on. Internet communication allows you and your team to connect without having to leave your offices.

4 Improves work relationships

Building a good relationship between workers spread around the globe is not easy. Business trips can negatively affect life– work balance. Team members can burn out fast if they have to make business travels that deny them the chance to participate in crucial events with friends and family. With internet communication, employees can effortlessly communicate with one another at anytime from anywhere in the world. This allows employees situated in different parts of the world to give their opinion and voice their concerns. Therefore, internet communication is an important business asset, particularly for companies that have tapped into global markets.

5 Increases productivity

While the companies of yesteryear might not have treasured effective communication, modern workplace requires both the management and the staff have the tools to effectively communicate internally and externally. This is because effective communication is important in increasing productivity as it directly impacts the behavior of the employees and how they perform. Internet communication plays an integral role in getting stuff done fast and efficiently which ultimately improves productivity. Poor communication can have a negative effect on productivity as the staff may not get the adequate info to accomplish a job they have been assigned.

6 Increases accountability

Errors slow down productivity and so it is tempting to punish or fire employees who repeatedly make errors. One major advantage of internet communication is that it helps to decrease these errors. This piece of technology pinpoints errors and how staff can avoid them. In workplaces that don't make use of various forms of internet communication, those mistakes go unnoticed. With internet communication, there is no room for mistakes as employees feel liable for their actions and safe to point out mistakes. They also feel secure expressing their ideas and suggestions in a group setting.

● Why does internet improvement can help any industries services or efficiencies improvment?

Internet improvement will revolutionize the world and lead to groundbreaking changes in transportation, industry, communication, education, energy, health care, communication, entertainment, government, warfare and even basic research. For example, self-driving cars, trains, semi-trucks, ships and airplanes will mean that goods and people can be transported farther, faster and with less energy and with massively fewer vehicles. Automated mining and manufacturing will further reduce the need for human workers to engage in rote work. Machine language translation will finally close the language barrier, while digital tutors, teachers and personal assistants with human qualities will make everything from learning new subjects to booking salon appointments faster and easier. For businesses, automated secretaries, salespeople, waiters, waitress, baristas and customer support personnel will lead to cost savings, efficiency gains and improved customer experiences. Socially, individuals will be able to find AI pets, friends and even therapists who can provide the love and emotional support that many people so desperately want. Entertainment will become far more interactive, as immersive AI experiences come to supplement traditional passive forms of media. Energy generation and health care will vastly improve with the addition of powerful AI tools that can take a systems-level view of operations and locate opportunities to gain efficiencies in design and operation. AI-driven robotics (e.g., drones) will revolutionize warfare. Finally, intelligent AI will contribute immensely to basic research and likely begin to create scientific discoveries of its own. So, it implies that internet improvement ought assist any kinds of industy service or efficiency improvement.

● Internet may become any organizational digital assets

On an individual basis, we will think about our digital assets as much as our physical ones. Ideally, we will have more transparent control over our data, and the ability to understand where it resides and exchange it for value – negotiating with the platform companies that are now in a winner-take-all position. Some children born today are named with search engine-optimization in mind; we'll be thinking more comprehensively about a set of rights and responsibilities of personal data that children are born with. Governments will have a higher level of regulation and protection of individual data. On an individual level, there will be greater integration of technology with our physical selves. For example, I can see devices that augment hearing and vision, and that enable greater access to data through our physical selves. Hard for me to picture what that looks like, but 50 years is a lot of time to figure it out. On a societal level, AI will have affected many jobs. Not only the truck drivers and the factory workers, but professions that have been largely unassailable – law, medicine – will have gone through a painful transformation. It seems entirely reasonable that a great deal of our digital lives will be focused on habitable environments: identifying them, improving them, expanding them.

Significant, often highly communication and computation technologically driven, advances in day-to-day areas like health care, safety and human services, will continue to have a significant measurable improvement in many lives, often 'invisible' as an unnoticed reduction in bad outcomes, will continue to reduce the incidence of human-scale disasters. Advances in opportunities for self-actualisation through education, community and creative work will continue. So, I believe that future many organizations may apply internet communication tool for their digital assets.

● Internet improvement may assist robotic development

Most of the focus on technology and particularly AI and machine learning developments these days is limited to virtual systems (e.g., apps for travel booking, social networks, search engines, games). I expect this to move, in the next 50 years, into networking people with machines, remotely operating in a myriad of environments, such as homes, hospitals, factories, sport arenas and so on. This will change work as we know it today, as it will change medicine (increasing remote surgery), travel (autonomous and remotely-guided cars, trains, planes), entertainment (games where real robots, instead of virtual agents, evolve in real scenarios). These are just a few ideas/scenarios. Many more, difficult to anticipate today, will appear. They will bring further challenges on privacy, security and safety, which everyone should be closely watching and monitoring. Beyond current discussions on privacy problems concerning 'virtual world' apps, we need to consider that 'real world' apps may enhance many of those problems, as they interact physically and/or in proximity with humans. So, future historians will observe that, in many ways, the rise of the internet over the next few decades will have improved the world, but it hasn't been without its costs that were sometimes severe and disruptive to entire industries and nations as well as improve robotic development.

This is similarly valid for AI.Living longer and better lives is the shining promise of the digital age. Many respondents to this canvassing agreed that internet advancement is likely to lead to better human-health outcomes, although perhaps not for everyone. As the following comments show, experts foresee new cures for chronic illnesses, rapid advancement in biotechnology and expanded access to care thanks to the development of better telehealth systems. Life will improve in multiple ways. One in particular I think worth mentioning will be improvements in health care in three distinct ways. One is significantly better medical technology related to cancer and other major diseases. The second is significantly reduced cost of health care. The third is much higher and broader availability of high-quality health care, thereby reducing the differences in outcomes between wealthy and poor citizens. So, when hospitals can improve internet communication , if the hospital can apply robots to assist doctors and nurses to serve patients. Then, internet communication can help them to cooperate more efficient.

● Internet improvement to assist 5G laptop development

Many of the technologies we see commercialized today began in government and university research labs. Fifty years ago, computers were the size of walk-in closets, and the notion of personal computers was laughable to most people. Today we're facing another shift, from personal and mobile to ambient computing. We're also seeing a huge amount of research in the areas of prosthetics, neuroscience and other technologies intended to translate brain activity into physical form. All discussion of transhumanism aside, there are very real current and future applications for technology 'implants' and prosthetics that will be able to aid mobility, memory, even intelligence, and other physical and neurological functions. And, as nearly always happens, the technology is far ahead of our understanding of the human implications. Will these technologies be available to all, or just to a privileged class? What happens to the data? Will it be 'willed' as a digital legacy to future generations? What are the ethical (and for some, religious and spiritual) implications of changing the human body with technology? In many ways, these are not new questions. We've used technology to augment the physical form since the first caveman picked up a walking stick. But the key here will be to focus as much (or more) on the way we use these technologies as we do on inventing them. All of above factors will be influenced to future 5G mobile phone by internet improvement?

Our homes, transportation, appliances, communication devices and even our clothes will be constantly communicating as part of a digital network. We have enough pieces of this today that we can somewhat imagine what it will be like. Through our clothes, doctors can monitor in real time our vital signs, metabolic condition and markers relevant to specific diseases. Parents will have real-time information about young children. The difference in the future will be the constant sharing of information, data updates and responses of all these interconnected devices. The things we create will interact with us to protect us. Our notions of privacy and even liability will be redefined. Lowering the cost and increasing the effectiveness of health care will require sharing information about how our bodies are functioning. Those who opt out may have to accept palliative hospice care over active treatment. Not keeping track of children real-time may be considered a form of child neglect. Digital will do more than connect our things to each other – it will invade our bodies. Advances in prosthetics, replacement organs and implants will turn our bodies into digital devices. This will create a host of new issues, including defining 'human' and where the line exists between that human and the digital universe – if people are always connected, always on are humans now part of the internet?

● How internet improvement influences AI provides medical service to hospitals?

Similarly, AI embedded in devices or wearables can be applied to predict and ameliorate many mental health illnesses. However, there is potential for there to be huge inequalities in our societies in the ability of individuals to access such technologies, causing both social disruption and new causes for mental health diseases, such as depression and anxiety. On balance, I am an optimist about the ability of human beings to adjust and develop new ethical norms for dealing with such issues.Surveillance technology, especially that powered by AI algorithms, is becoming more powerful and all-present than ever before. But to look at that and say that technology won't help people is absurd. Medical technology, technology to help people with disabilities, technology that will increase our comfort and abilities as humans will continue to appear and develop.The digital revolution will bring benefits in particular for health, providing personalized monitoring through Internet of Things and wearable devices. The AI will analyze those data in order to provide personalized medicine solutions.The most noticeable change for better in the next 50 years will be in health and average life expectancy. At this pace, and, taking into account the developments in digital technologies, I hope that several discoveries will reduce the risk of death, such as cancer or even death by road accident. New drugs could be developed, increasing the active work age and possibility maintaining the sustainability of countries' social health care and retirement funds. Another area AI can have impact is in creating the framework within genomics, epigenomics and metabolomics can be used to keep people healthy and to intervene when we start to deviate from health. Indeed, with AI we may be able to hack the brain and other secreting cells so that we can auto-generate lifesaving medicines, block unwanted biological processes (e.g., cancer), and coupled to understanding the brain, be able to hack at neurological disorders."

Thus, I believe that future hospitals were able to utilize internet technology to solve human health problems to make citizens' lives better and improve their access to care and services to improve their health outcomes. The benefits of the internet in the health care industry have continued to improve access to care and services, particularly for elderly, disabled or rural citizens. Digital tools will continue to be integrated into daily life to help the most vulnerable and isolated who need services, care and support. With laws supporting these groups, benefits in these areas will continue and expand to include behavioral health and resources for this group and for others. In the area of behavioral health in particular, digital tools will provide far-reaching benefits to citizens who need services but do not access them directly in person. Access to behavioral health will increase significantly in the next 50 years as a result of more enhanced and widely available digital tools made available to practitioners for delivering care to vulnerable populations, and by minimizing the stigma of accessing this type of care in person. It is a more affordable, personalized and continuous way of providing this type of care that is also more likely to attain adherence.

● The cyborg generation: Humans will partner more directly with technology when internet is popular to be used in any where

The inevitable 'Singularity' will result in changes to humans and will increase the rate of our evolution toward hybrid 'machines.' I also believe that new and modified materials will become 'smart.' For instance, new materials will be 'self-aware' and will be able to communicate problems in order to avoid failure. Ultimately, these materials will become 'self-healing' and will be able to harness raw materials to manufacture replacement parts in situ. All these materials, and the things built with them will participate in the connected world. We will see continued blurring of the line between 'real' and 'virtual' life." For exaple, artificial general intelligence and quantum computing available in a future version of the cloud connected to individual brain augmentation could make us augmented geniuses, inventing our daily lives in a self-actualization economy as the conscious-technology civilization evolves. Implants in humans that continuously connect them to the web will lead to a loss of privacy and the potential for thought control, decline in autonomy.

● Everyone agrees that the world will be putting AI to work, when internet is improvement to raise robotic efficiency and performance improvement

The technology visionaries surveyed described a much different work environment from the current one. They say remote work arrangements are likely to be the rule, rather than the exception, and virtual assistants will handle many of the mundane and unpleasant tasks currently performed by humans. The shooting is done by a drone guided by a smart guy/gal working a 9-to-5 job in an air-conditioned office in a nice town. Garbage could be picked up, sorted, recycled, all by robots with AI. Tedious surgery completed by robots and teaching via YouTube would leave the humans to the interesting and exciting cases, not the redoing of same lessons to yet more patients/students. Humans could live well on a 20-hour work week with many weeks of paid vacation. Having a job/career could become a positive, not just a necessity. With 24/7 learning and just-in-time capacity, people could change areas or careers many times with ease whenever they become bored. This positive outcome is possible if we collectively manage the creation and distribution of the tools and access to the use of new emerging tools. Thus, future everyone will have hundreds of digital workers working for them. Our cognitive mediators will know us in some ways better than we know ourselves. Better episodic memories and large numbers of digital workers will allow expanded entrepreneurship, lifelong learning and focus on transformation.

Thus, our future social development already small world will shrink further as remote collaboration becomes the norm, resulting in major social changes, among them allowing the recent concentration of expertise in major cities to relax and reducing the relevance of national borders. Furthermore, deep learning and AI-assisted technologies for software development and verification, combined with more abstract primitives for executing software in the cloud, will enable even those not trained as software engineers to precisely describe and solve complex problems. I believe the question we're facing is not 'When will machines surpass human intelligence?' but instead 'How can humans work together with machines in new ways?' Rather than worrying about an impending Singularity, I propose the concept of Multiplicity: where diverse combinations of people and machines work together to solve problems and innovate. In analogy with the 1910 High School Movement that was spurred by advances in farm automation, I propose a 'Multiplicity Movement' to evolve the way we learn to emphasize the uniquely human skills that AI and robots cannot replicate: creativity, curiosity, imagination, empathy, human communication, diversity and innovation. AI systems can provide universal access to sophisticated adaptive testing and exercises to discover the unique strengths of each student and to help each student amplify his or her strengths. AI systems could support continuous learning for students of all ages and abilities. Rather than discouraging the human workers of the world with threats of an impending Singularity, let's focus on Multiplicity where advances in AI and robots can inspire us to think deeply about the kind of work we really want to do, how we can change the way we learn and how we might embrace diversity to create myriad new partnerships. So, future AI and internet technoloy will become new partners to assist any business development, even any organizations and social development. Hence, internet improvement must be needed in order to let any businesses can apply robots to raise efficiencies and improve performance more effectively. For example, free internet-connected devices will be available to the poor in exchange for carrying around a sensor that records traffic speed, environmental quality, detailed usage logs, and video and audio recordings (depending on state law). There will be secure vote-by-internet capabilities, through credit card or passport verification, with other secure kiosks available at public facilities (police stations, libraries, fire stations and post offices, should those continue to exist in their current form). Internet and 24/7 real-time connectivity will no longer be viewed as a 'thing' independent from daily life, but integral, like electricity. This has profound psychological implications about what people assume as normal and establishes baseline expectations for access, response times and personalization of functions and information. Contrary to many concerns, as technology becomes more sophisticated, it will ultimately support the primary human drives of social connectedness and agency. As we have seen with social media, first adoption is noncritical – it is a shiny penny for exploration. Then people start making judgments about the value-add based on their own goals and technology companies adapt by designing for more value to the user . Technology is going to change whether we like it or not – expecting it to be worse for individuals means that we look for what's wrong. Expecting it to be better means we look for the strengths and what works and work toward that goal. Technology gives individuals more control – a fundamental human need and a prerequisite to participatory citizenship and collective agency. The danger is that we are so distracted by technology that we forget that digital life is an extension of the offline world and demands the same critical, moral and ethical thinking.

In future 50 years every aspect of our life will be connected, organized and hence, partly controlled, as technology platform and applications businesses will take this opportunity. A few global players will dominate the business; smaller companies (startups) will mostly have a chance in the development sector. Many institutions, such as libraries, will disappear – there might be one or two libraries that function as museums to show how it used to be. People who experienced today's world will definitely value the benefits and amenities they have through technology (human-machine/AI collaboration). If technology becomes part of every aspect of our lives we will have to give up some power and control. People thinking in today's terms will lose a certain amount of freedom, independency and control over their lives. People born after 2030 will probably just think these technologies produced changes that are mostly for the better. It has always been like this – people have always thought/said 'in the old days everything was better. The free, open internet that represented a set of decentralized connections between idiosyncratic actors will be recognized as an aberration in the history of the internet. Today's internet giants will probably be the internet giants of 50 years from now. In recent years, they've made substantial progress in curtailing innovation through acquisitions and copying. As the industry matures, they will add regulatory capture to their skill sets. For many people around the world, the internet will be a set of narrow portals where they exchange their data for a curtailed set of communication, information and consumer services. Thus, digital tools will be part of our body inside and remotely, and will assist us in decision- making constantly, so it will become second nature. Nonetheless, physical feelings will still be exclusively 'physical,' i.e., there will be a significant difference between the 'sensor-based feelings' and real body feelings, so human beings will still have some advantages over technology. This, I believe, will last forever.

CHAPTER SIX

Discovery new health medicine drugs

Why do we need to concern new health medicine drugs discovery? I believe that human will face any new kinds of diseases that we had not encountered or contacts in my past. If we lack any new kinds of health medicine drugs discovery to fight any kinds of new diseases in my future. Then, we must face death very easily, such as COVID 19 is one kind of new disease, the another person or other persons can be contacted to cause this kind of COVID 19 disease by the patient's cloths, shoes, hands, even air, mouth of hs body and things. Thus, it had caused many people die in global nowadays. So, medicine or drug or bio-scientists need to spend much time to do any experiment to attempt to discover any new kinds of medicines or drugs to fight any future new kinds of diseases. Otherwise, human will die very easily in soon.

● Why do we need drug discovery?

In the fields of medicine, biotechnology and pharmacology, drug discovery is the process by which new candidate medications are discovered. Historically, drugs were discovered by identifying the active ingredient from traditional remedies or by serendipitous discovery, as with penicillin. More recently, chemical libraries of synthetic small molecules, natural products or extracts were screened in intact cells or whole organisms to identify substances that had a desirable therapeutic effect in a process known as classical pharmacology. After sequencing of the human genome allowed rapid cloning and synthesis of large quantities of purified proteins, it has become common practice to use high throughput screening of large compounds libraries against isolated biological targets which are hypothesized to be disease-modifying in a process known as reverse pharmacology. Hits from these screens are then tested in cells and then in animals for efficacy.

However, modern drug discovery involves the identification of screening hits, medicinal chemistry and optimization of those hits to increase the affinity, selectivity (to reduce the potential of side effects), efficacy/potency, metabolic stability (to increase the half-life), and oral bioavailability. Once a compound that fulfills all of these requirements has been identified, the process of drug development can continue. If successful, clinical trials are developed. Modern drug discovery is thus usually a capital-intensive process that involves large investments by pharmaceutical industry corporations as well as national governments (who provide grants and loan guarantees). Despite advances in technology and understanding of biological systems, drug discovery is still a lengthy, "expensive, difficult, and inefficient process" with low rate of new therapeutic discovery. For example, in 2010, the research and development cost of each new molecular entity was about US$1.8 billion In the 21st century, basic discovery research is funded primarily by governments and by philanthropic organizations, while late-stage development is funded primarily by pharmaceutical companies or venture capitalists. However, discovering drugs that may be a commercial success, or a public health success, involves a complex interaction between investors, industry, academia, patent laws, regulatory exclusivity, marketing and the need to balance secrecy with communication. Meanwhile, for disorders whose rarity means that no large commercial success or public health effect can be expected, the orphan drug funding process ensures that people who experience those disorders can have some hope of pharmacotherapeutic advances.

● Where do new drugs come from? Why does it take so long to get a new drug approved? Why are drugs so expensive?

The medicines we ingest, inject, and inhale are often complex therapeutic compounds. The drugs are usually mixtures of chemicals made from starting materials or drug sources. Depending on the sources from which the drugs were created, the drugs can be categorized as natural, synthetic, or semi-synthetic. Natural drugs are made from compounds found in nature. The most prevalent natural drug sources are plants. The field of science that studies the relationship between people and medicinal plants is known as medicinal ethnobotany. Some examples of medicine that come from plants are morphine (from opium), digoxin (from flower, Digitalis lanata), and aspirin (from willow tree bark). Less prevalent natural drug sources include animals, microbes, and minerals. The first kind drug source is for example, synthetic drugs come from starting materials that are not found in nature. Instead, they are produced by man from smaller chemical building blocks. An example of synthetic medicine is the experimental antimalaria drug, arterolane. Another kind drug source is semi-synthetic drugs are neither completely natural nor completely synthetic. They are a hybrid. Semi-synthetic drugs are generally made by converting starting materials from natural sources into final products via chemical reactions. Examples of semi-synthetic medicine include the antibiotic, penicillin, and the chemotherapy drug, paclitaxel. To make the chemotherapy drug, paclitaxel, 10-deacetylbaccatin is extracted from yew needles and undergoes a 4-stage synthesis process. They both are the main kinds of drugs manufacturing sources.

● Why does human need new drugs discovery ?

The reason of global health needs demand new approach to drug discovery, the pharmaceutical industry has made enormous strides in the production of potential therapies and medicines. But even today, close to 90% of candidate drugs that enter Phase 1 trials fail to make it to the market place. This is a system beset by duplication of effort and hence wastage of resources. No one lab or institution can do this on its own. We must urgently pool resources and expertise, minimise duplication, explore new drug targets, biomarkers, and technologies in order to generate new, effective, and more affordable drugs for patients more quickly.

Discovey of any one kind of new drug, it needs long time to experiment. It must come up with new ways to accelerate our drug discovery process. Alternatively, we must entirely rethink how we treat illness. This is not just limited to bacterial infections. We need to invent better ways to combat all forms of disease. The process of discovering, testing, and approving a drug for commercial use can take 20 years and over of 1 billion dollars. Obviously, decreasing both the time and the cost of developing these drugs can save many lives. There are some new technologies which are already helping to ramp up this process. For example, computational modeling of drugs has massively sped up the screening process for drugs. We can now take thousands of potential drug candidates and narrow them down to a couple viable options. But there are more ways we can expedite this process.

A recent estimate states that we now know the molecular cause of over 4,000 diseases — but we only have drugs for about 250. How can we do better? The FDA approval process is long and arduous. Even for compounds that have been approved in other countries, FDA trials can be drawn out for years. The FDA approval process can be responsible for about 25% of the cost of a drug and can delay the arrival of a drug over 10 years. There is even data that suggests that the FDA kills many more by not approving drugs than it ever saves by approving drugs (for more on the harmful effects of the FDA, see Cato, Forbes, The Independent Institute, and LifeExtension). By delaying good drugs that can save lives, and by doing little to stop bad drugs, the FDA is often an inhibitor to the medical process. We need to rethink the FDA if we want to streamline the drug discovery process. If we can change many FDA policies, we will see more drugs created for those 4,000 known targets.

● The process of new drug experiment success time evaluation

Any new kind of drugs experiment success, they must experience these processes. They may include:

1 Drug testing and licensing

All new drugs and treatments have to be thoroughly tested before they are licensed and available for patients. A new drug is first studied in the laboratory. If it looks promising, it is carefully studied in people. If trials show that it works well and doesn't cause too many side effects, it may be licensed. You may hear this process called 'from bench to bedside. There is no typical length of time it takes for a drug to be tested and approved. It might take 10 to 15 years or more to complete all 3 phases of clinical trials before the licensing stage. But this time span varies a lot. There are many factors that affect how long it takes for a drug to be licensed.

2 Factors that affect how long trials take

The type of cancer drug success experiement needs time

Clinical trials for rarer cancers often take longer because there are fewer patients available to take part. Research teams from several different countries may need to collaborate so there are enough patients. This can mean the trial takes longer to organise and set up. But international trials can often recruit people more quickly and so are likely be quicker in the long run.

Researchers running clinical trials for more common cancers are generally able to find enough people to take part more easily.

3 The type of treatment

Trials that use new methods of giving treatment, such as a new way to give radiotherapy for example, may take longer to set up and run. This is because the research teams need specialist equipment and extra training. These trials may only be able to run in a small number of hospitals compared to trials using standard ways of giving treatment. How long treatment takes can also affect the results. It is likely to be quicker to get results for a trial looking at a single dose or short course of treatment, compared to a treatment that lasts for months or even years.

4 The type of trial

Some trials look at treatments to prevent cancer or ways of screening for cancer. Screening means testing for cancer in people who don't have any signs or symptoms. People who join these trials haven't been diagnosed with cancer. The research team will often want to follow them for many years to see who develops cancer and who doesn't. They will then compare the different trial groups to see if a particular treatment can help prevent cancer or whether a test can help to diagnose it early.These trials often take a long time to get results compared to treatment trials. It can take years to see a clear difference in the number of people in the different groups who go on to develop cancer. So, any new kinds of drug research experiements, they depend on the number of patients needed in order to decide whether how drug quality level, how many drugs manufacturing supply number, drug price in global market.

Statistics experts look at what the research team want to find out and the design of the trial, and then work out how many patients are needed. If there aren't enough patients taking part, the results may not be reliable. The number of people they need to get reliable results will depend on how many treatment groups there are and exactly what the research team want to find out.

5 The follow up period

Research teams look at how well people are doing for some time after they have treatment as part of a trial. This is to see how well the treatment works over a longer period of time, and to find out more about long term side effects. Follow up periods can range from a few months to more than 10 years, depending on the type of treatment and the group of patients. Or maybe longer for a trial looking at screening or prevention.

6 Any problems with the new treatment

There may be problems with new drugs or treatments that the researchers don't know about until they run the trials. There could be unexpected side effects or reactions to treatment. Or there may be difficulties in giving the treatment to patients. Problems with the new treatment may mean the trial takes longer to complete.

Thus, any kinds of new drug experiement need long time to be attempted to carry on, every new kind of drug experiment is evaluated about 10 to 20 , even more time. So, future drug scientists have responsibilities to evaluate whether which kinds of diseases will cause in order to concentrate on spending time to carry on researching the kind of new drug experiment. It aims to use limited resource and time to let patients to get health.

CHAPTER SEVEN

Improving living environment

What are the disadvantages if we do not concern how to improve our global living environment? I shall explain as below:

● reasons to improve living environment

Nowadays, as population on the earth keeps expanding, human needs increase endlessly causing more global environmental problems to proliferate globally. Global environmental crisis has become an unequivocal fact that can affect our livelihood and it is capable of changing the current landscape drastically. Hence, people hold the responsibility to tackle current global environmental issues to make this world a better place. With destructive natural disasters like flash floods or snowstorm as well as the changing of weather patterns, the earth is poised at the precarious verge of severe environmental crisis. Human intervention has caused many dysfunctions to the environment, some of which have left damages on the ecosystem that eliminates other sources of necessity to other living things. Ever since humans start to harvest the Earth 's resources, many landscapes have been altered to fit the lifestyles of countless inhabitants. So people ought to be aware of other types of environmental challenges that the planet is facing. Some of the challenges that the planet is facing include overpopulation of human beings that leads to natural resources depletion, deforestation and loss of biodiversity, acid rain and ocean acidification, pollution and waste disposal. Thus, it seems that global living environment and pollution have close relationship. I mean that air and water and paste and chemical pollution will reduce if we can keep our global living environment more clean, safe and without more rubblishs are allowed to keep in our living places, even gardens, public places anywhere.

One of the key ethical questions is whether a life-extension pill would extend our healthy years or simply prolong frailty towards the end of life. Better health and longer life would certainly be an attractive prospect for many people. If we were healthier for longer then perhaps we could achieve more of our ambitions and engage in the things we enjoy for longer. But some people worry that our lives may be extended in a state of low quality of life rather than health. Although this is not the goal, critics worry that it might be an unintended consequence of intervention in ageing and longevity. As with all pharmaceuticals, both health benefits and risks need to be considered. If life span could be extended a great deal – perhaps to more than 100 years or even longer – then some other interesting issues might arise. For instance, would we simply run out of things to do and become bored? Even things that we enjoy may become stale after several centuries. How long would we have to work for? If our lives were 200 years long then it is unlikely that many people could afford to retire at 65. However, this may also present new opportunities such as having several different careers within a lifetime. If our future earth can not provide a health and clean living environment to let human to live, then our quality of living must be worse to compare nowadays, it will cause our next generation can not be health to live ot they will have many different kinds of disease, such as COV19 disease , or future there are many kinds of serious disease to compare COV19 disease , they will bring threats to influence our next generation to live in anywhere health places in our earth. It is very disappointment to us, such as our next generation's parents, we have not feel responsibilities to keep our living environment to be improved to let our next generation to live in global anywhere clean and health living environment. So, we need to concern how to improve our living environment nowadays.

However, I shall suggest these methods how to improve our living environment to be better. If we can be habit to do environment protection behaviors every day, then our living environment must be influenced to improve more easily and rapidly, in society, individual sand businessmen and our governments have resposibilities, they may include as below:

● Individual and businessmen and governments how to improve living environment

Individual responsibilities to improving living environment

1. Use Reusable Bags

Plastic grocery-type bags that get thrown out end up in landfills or in other parts of the environment. These can suffocate animals who get stuck in them or may mistake them for food. Also, it takes a while for the bags to decompose. Whether you are shopping for food, clothes or books, use a reusable bag. This cuts down on litter and prevents animals from getting a hold of them. There are even some stores (such as Target) that offer discounts for using reusable bags! These bags are useful for things other than shopping as well. I have heard of people using reusable bags when they move! If you forget your bags at home, buy a new one. Better yet, keep a couple bags in your car so you never leave home without them (just make sure you remember you put them there)! If you are in a position where you need to use the plastic bags, reuse them the next time you go shopping, or use them for something else. Just do not be so quick to throw them out!

There are some states that are outlawing or charging extra for using plastic bags. Using reusable bags helps the environment AND your budget!

2. Print as Little as Necessary

We have all had that teacher that wanted us to have a copy of every single reading when we come to class, or that professor who wanted a hard copy of the ten-page paper that is due next week. These are fine but it seems as if they do not understand that using so much paper is detrimental to the environment. What can you do? Ask your teacher if you can bring a laptop or an e-reader to class so that you can download the reading onto that and read it from there. If not, print on both sides of the page to reduce the amount of paper used. If you need to turn in a long paper, ask the professor if it is okay to print on both sides of the page and explain why you're asking. Most teachers care about the environment as well and would be willing to allow you to do so.

3. Recycle

Recycling is such a simple thing to do, but so many people don't do it. Many garbage disposal companies offer recycling services, so check with the company you use to see if they can help you get started! It is as simple as getting a bin and putting it out with your trash cans for free!

Another way to recycle is to look for recycling cans near trashcans. Instead of throwing recyclables in the trash with your non-recyclables, make a point to take an extra step to locate recycling cans around your campus.

4. Use a Reusable Beverage Containers

Instead of buying individually-packaged drinks, consider buying a bulk container of the beverage you want and buying a reusable water bottle. Not only will this help the environment, but it will also help you save money since you are buying a bulk container. Many campuses offer water fountains designed for drinking as well as for refilling reusable water bottles. Make use of these fountains throughout the day when you finish off the initial beverage. Along these lines, many restaurants offer reusable containers for drinks. If you go to a certain place a lot, consider buying one of these containers to help minimize waste. A lot of coffee shops even offer a discount to customers who use a reusable container for their drinks. Starbucks, as an example, offers a small discount for customers who do this. Saving the environment and money?

5. Save Water

Water is wasted more frequently than we can see. Turn off the faucet as you are brushing your teeth. Don't turn your shower on until you're ready to get in and wash your hair. Limit your water usage as you wash dishes. Changing old habits will be good for both the environment and your wallet!

6. Avoid Taking Cars or Carpool When Possible

Cars are harmful to the environment. Taking public transportation, walking, or riding a bike to class are better options that help the environment and your budget, as well as getting some exercise in! If you do need to use your car, compare schedules and places of residency with those in your classes. You can split the cost of gas and have alternating schedules for who drives when. This is cheaper than everyone driving separately and you'll be closer with friends!

Businessmen responsibilities to improving living environment

Instead of individuals have respobsibilities to improve our living environment. Businessmen have also responsibilities to improve our living environment. I shall indicate mining businessmen example to explain how mining businesses may influence our living environment to be worse. The disadvantages of mining include harm to air pollution, water pollution, loss of usable land, destruction of animal habitat, and harm to local communities and the miners themselves. While mining produces the resources needed for fuel, electronics, and other items as well as jobs, companies often don't factor the harm mining can do into their decision making. Below factors may influence our global living environment to be worse as below:

Air Pollution

Lead, arsenic, cadmium, and other harmful substance As are often exposed by mining and picked up by the wind, causing allergies and breathing problems in local people. Mining machinery uses fossil fuels and releases large amounts of carbon dioxide and other substances that contribute to global warming.

Water Pollution

Mining can cause metal contamination and acid mine drainage that makes water unsafe for plants and animals. Sediments released by mining choke streams and erode soil. Both of these problems also cause problems for farming and the water people drink.

Loss of Usable Land

Mining, especially open pit mining, destroys land that can be used for farming, houses, and other human purposes, often permanently. Entire mountains and rivers can be destroyed. Loss of soil and deep underground excavation can also make land unstable and collapse.

Destruction of Animal Habitats

Mining also has disadvantages for plants and wildlife. It destroys homes and food sources for animals and leads to less diverse plant and animal life. Endangered species that are already sensitive to changes in their environment are especially at risk. Because mining releases toxins that linger for years later, the damage to plants and animals often isn't fully understood until after mining has ended.

Harm to Miners

Mining is dangerous for the people who do it, especially for miners who work underground. Breathing in mineral dust can cause deadly diseases like pneumoconiosis or black lung, while the machinery used often causes hearing loss. Back injuries and other physical problems are also common in miners. While big disasters often show up in the news, many of the miners who are killed or injured on the job never receive media attention. In 2010, almost 2,500 miners died from causes other than major accidents.

Consequences for Local Communities

Mining is also harmful to the communities that support mines. Mining can lead to loss of homes, land, and clean water, and it often releases chemicals into the environment that cause health problems for locals. Mines also need large amounts of water to operate, which leaves less for people to drink or farm with. It also causes less obvious problems. Because only some people in an area benefit from mining, but everyone faces at least some of the disadvantages, mining can divide communities. It can also lead to harassment or abuse from corporate or government officials who care more about the profits of mining than the people it affects. The secrecy around mining and who makes money from it often makes this disadvantage even worse.

Thus, ourselves and businessmen can not neglect our any activities can influence global living environment to be worse. We need to learn how to avoid to do any bad behaviors to influence our future global living environment to be worse, even the worst.

Governments responsibilities to improving living environment

Any country's government needs to concern social responsibility before it decides to implement any sustainable development. Because although sustainable development may bring some benefits to some countries, but it can also bring disadvantages to themselves countries. What Are Disadvantages of Sustainable Development? It may brins these disadvantages as below:

Increased Costs

Because sustainable development relies on newer technologies and materials that cost more to produce, the overall costs are often more than that of traditional construction. The higher cost of materials is passed on to developers. Developers pass it on to property owners, who pass it on to tenants. Future development will include tools that haven't even been invented yet. The trial and error of using new materials and ideas can also bring costs up for everyone.

Lower Quality of Life for Some Elements of Society

Sustainable development will shrink or do away with certain job sectors. This will lead to job loss for some workers. The fossil fuel industry could see plants close and employees lose jobs as sustainable development relies on new energy sources. The rising costs and less robust power of alternative energy can also lead to a lower quality of life for people who live in sustainably developed areas.

Resistance to New Methods

When people try to implement new ideas, there's naturally a certain amount of resistance. People in general are set in their ways and don't want to change their lives radically. As more governments and companies attempt to put sustainable development into practice, more resistance will follow.

Some of the resistance will come in the form of people who initially adopt the idea of sustainable development with enthusiasm, but their commitment shrinks as they start to put new ideas into practice. Contractors and tenants may resist a specific initiative because it forces them to change the ways they work and live.

Increased Regulation

Sustainable approaches will naturally lead to increased regulation on construction and the daily operation of businesses. A greater commitment to the environment will lead to tighter controls on how people live their lives. Stricter building codes and tougher emission standards are likely. While some people will accept a greater burden of regulation because they see the overall benefit, many people will disagree with government intruding into their lives.

Political Struggle

In addition to the public resistance, there's a political cost to committing to the environment. The deep political divides in society mean that some political powers won't want to commit to sustainable initiatives. Certain industries will try to influence politicians via lobbyists. Some politicians will be completely against sustainable development.

Is It Worth the Trouble?

People and organizations that are in favor of sustainable development believe that it's worth moving past these disadvantages to work on the environment. Advocates say that sustainable development is an investment in future generations. The biggest defenders of these initiatives are working on ways of overcoming the hurdles.

Thus, ineffective or poor sustainable development may also bring poor living environment, due to wrong sustainable development to the country. For example, if Afria government only concern how to find mining lands for sustinable development, but it neglects to keep clean and health and natural land living environment to African to continue to live. Then, it will reduce African quality of living to be worse. So, any countries governments need to keep balance to bring social benefit when they decide to do sustainable development in themselves countries.

CHAPTER EIGHT

Improving social welfare

Do you feel our nowadays social welfare is enough? What factors can influence our social welfare to be better or worse? Do we need to improve our social welfare to let our next generations feel comfortable and without difficulty to live? What feeling will influence to our future next generation if we do not plan to improve our social welfare? I shall explain why we need to concern how to improve our social welfare in order to let our next generation won't difficult to live as below:

● Why do we improve future social welfare ?

Why do we need to improve social welfare? Firstly, I shall explain why we need social welfare. Then, I shall explain why we need to improve social welfare. Social welfare may be explained that it is one kind of social protection has the potential to reduce insecurity for workers and help to bring employment contracts. Also, it is an investment in human capital for economic growth as successful economic depend on the quality of their workforce.

Why do we need social welfare? As a social welfare system offers assistance to individuals and families in need with such program as health care assistance, food providing and unemployment compensation. Lesser knon pasts of a social welfare system include disaster reief and educational assistances. What is the importance of welfare? When the welfare state has played aim important role to any countries in reducing socio-economic inequalities and proetcting people from various forms of handship , such as unemployment and ill health , as also proverty be an important social problem for economic development.

What is the purpose of social welfare policies? Social wefare policies mean providing especially assistance and social insurance benefit, traditionally have been conceived as instruments of social protection and redistribution. At a minimum, social welfare policies should protect individuals form proverty and relative deprivations So, it brings this question: who benefits from social welfare? The most common types of programs provide benefits to the elderly or retired, the sick or invalid, dependent survivors, mothers, the unemployed, the work-injured, and families. Methods of financing and administration and the scope of coverage and benefits vary widely among countries may be implemented in popular.

Nowadays, our societies believe that social welfare is an important tool for redistribution, social protection which has to be at the heart of the construction of the European project. If social and labour market policies are conceived in an appropriate manner, they help to promote both social justice and economic efficiency and productivity, instead of providing education, medical retired etc. welfare to the low income, low educational level social group as well as to achieve reducing poverty and inequality aim. Thus, it explains why our societies need to learn how to improve our global future social welfare to be be better , even the best social welfare system.

On conclusion, why was social welfare needed to create? Our society's population had been increasing rapidly and human's age had been prolonging, due to medical improvement, enough food provision. However, global has may dependent children and poor old people would gradually need as employment improved, retired assistance, unemployment assistance, educational assistance, and those over 65 age began to collect social security pensions. So, if we can not improve our societies to have the best social welfare to assist, these the most need of social assistance group. Consequently, the difference of rich and poor group must increase . It will be unfair to those low education and old age and low income families group in global. Thus, our future society must need to implement safe feeling to let anyone feel ourselves countries are suitable to us to live for our next generation. Hence, learning how to improve social welfare must be need to every country nowadays.

● Can improve social welfare to influence economy growth?

How social welfare impact any country itself economy? Does it has relationship between social welfare and economy? When it comes to public discourse the term "welfare state" is most often used in a derogatory way. For many people who hear the term welfare state, it means money being handed to people in poverty who don't deserve it because they aren't working to earn their income. The prevailing logic is that everyone knows hard workers are rewarded with higher income. However, that term means something different to actual economists who have dedicated their lives to studying economic systems and their impacts on broader society. In fact, the welfare state doesn't only apply to allocating resources to those living in poverty. It also means allocating resources to corporations. Any time the government allocates resources to any recipient in society, it is considered part of the welfare state. Capitalism lends itself naturally to economic cycles. The economy tends to swing severely between booms and busts. Without any kind of social insurance though, a capitalist economy may not recover from the bust end of a cycle. Even if it does, it would take much longer to recover than it would with social insurances in place. It is not in the best interest of the economy or society for a bust to last too long. The health of the economy is dependent on the economic health of the members of society.

However, Any type of government intervention is viewed as against a pure capitalist system. However, capitalism on paper has not worked out as well in practice without some government intervention on behalf of the greater good of society. Sometimes this has looked like a low level of resource distribution to those less fortunate and sometimes it has taken the form of resource distribution to corporations. Even an example such as farmers getting subsidies is a form of the welfare state. The guiding principle of welfare economics should be bringing all shareholders of the economy to a state of equilibrium where all groups share in the feeling of economic well-being.

However, the equilibrium doesn't happen all by itself. It requires public policy through government regulation and intervention to guide the economy in the direction of widespread well-being without sacrificing growth. Welfare economics can't end the bust end of the capitalist economic cycle. What it is meant to do, though, is mitigate the negative impacts of economic recessions. Welfare economics is meant to ensure that the bust end of the cycle isn't too severe and doesn't last too long. We should not be looking to cause undue economic suffering for any members of society.

I beleive that social welfare can impact economy growth. It means that the country can have better economy growth improvement, if it can provide good welfare to itself country. Otherwise, the country can have worse economy growth, if it can not provide good welfare to itself country. The reaons are becaure welfare can include any corporate (company) it's income as well as social individual both. There are two major types of welfare in the welfare state: social welfare and corporate welfare. While there are people in both types of welfare that do take advantage of the system, both are important tactics for stabilizing the economy.

1. Social Welfare

Social welfare encompasses programs such as social security, Medicare/Medicaid, food stamps, unemployment, the Affordable Care Act and other similar programs. The idea of these programs is to help safeguard people from poverty. The vast majority of the people who need to use these programs are either children, or they've worked their entire lives in our economic system. Fraud is extremely rare in these programs.

2. Corporate Welfare

Corporate welfare comes in a few different forms as well and is very much a type of welfare state. It is tax money that is given to corporations. It can also come in the form of tax cuts to corporations and it can also look like subsidies in certain industries. The purposes of using corporate welfare are usually to help grow a certain industry, to help stabilize a certain industry, or to help a certain industry avoid financial ruin. An example of corporate welfare is the auto-industry bailout. It is believed that corporate welfare actions such as these prevent an even worse economic disaster. Sometimes though, it seems corporate welfare moves make little sense. An example is the most recent Trump tax cuts. The economy has been growing for the past 8 years and is still doing well. Injecting government funds to booming industries through a corporate welfare action like the Trump tax cuts does not seem to fit any of the usual categories for stimulating the economy or preventing a downturn. It is unclear what the effects will be, but the move has been widely controversial among economists.

Hence, if the country has good social welfare system to provide itself country any company sale increasing chance. Then, when the country has many companies can earn high income, when many customers buy their products or consume their lesiure services. Consequently, the country's economy may be influenced to grow rapidly. The corporate welfare side of the welfare state can have some benefits. For instance, the automobile industry bailout saved jobs and a possible worse recession. By the government investing in budding renewable energy programs, it can generate economic growth in areas with innovative solutions to head off an energy crisis. Corporate welfare money doesn't always have that same effect on the economy. There should be greater scrutiny over how corporate welfare is used and whether it contributes significantly to economic growth. All corporate welfare programs should provide benefits to the whole economy.

On the other side, countries such as Norway have found that social welfare boosts their economies and capitalism.

Economics professors in Norway have discovered that despite the short-term sacrifice of providing higher wages for their upper-class citizens, in the long term their social welfare programs have resulted in better equality, smaller gender wage gaps, and improved education across the nation—just to name a few examples given by Science Nordic.

Do welfare states boost economic growth ? If in the future human labour is less needed, keeping societies stitched together may require us to reinvent the welfare state. The laws of economics say social welfare should be in accordance with the economic development level of a country. Welfare programs that are beyond a country's development level are not good for economic development, as has happened in Greece. On the other hand, if the economy develops rapidly without corresponding improvement in people's living standards and public welfare, people will not feel a "sense of gain", which in turn will have a negative impact on economic development.

First, excessive welfare beyond a country's development level will impede accumulation and harm welfare programs in the future. In economics, production is the top priority and it decides consumption. A society has to improve its production level if it wants to improve its consumption level. Production here refers to extended production, because only expanding the scale will breed competition and provide unfailing supply. The expansion of scale should be high-quality and high-level expansion of production through innovation and improvement of the industrial structure. Second, welfare at any level needs economic support. High levels of welfare in countries such as Sweden depend on high taxation and high deficit. But the high-level welfare in Greece depends on high debt. High welfare supported by high taxation reduces development funds for enterprises, impeding the development of enterprises. And if enterprises lose energy, the entire economy will suffer. High taxation also affects individuals' desire and capacity for consumption and thus undermines people's enthusiasm to expand production. Third, excessive welfare will breed dependence and result in waste of social resources. Although high welfare comes from individual taxpayers' contribution, it seems like a public welfare provided by the state. It will result in many social problems, such as waste of social resources, voluntarily unemployment and retirement in advance. Once people get used to this kind of dependence, economic development will be undermined. economic development will also be undermined if the authorities fail to provide enough welfare for the people.

For China economy development example, China social welfare and itself economy deveopment has exact close relationship. There is a lesson to be learned here from the planned economy to China economy growth and its social welfare can be improved nowadays. China's social welfare level today is not high; there is much room for improvement. So to strike the right balance between welfare and economic development, we should abide by the following principles:

One, it has to be clarified that the basic and final goal of China's economic development is the well-being of the Chinese people. And since China is the world's second-largest economy, it should pay more attention to improving public welfare. The Fifth Plenum of the 18th Communist Party of China Central Committee said the national GDP and urban and rural residents' incomes have to be doubled by 2020 compared with the 2010 level, and hence the authorities should focus on coordinated development to improve public services.

Two, the distribution of public welfare should be fair and transparent. The public welfare different social groups enjoy today is unbalanced, especially when it comes to urban and rural areas. Therefore, the authorities should make efforts to rectify the imbalance.

Three, the authorities should take measures to prevent unfairness and corruption from creeping into redistribution of welfare.

And four, they should not forget that China is still a developing country, and development is key to solving social economic problems, and only further development can guarantee sustainable and high-level welfare. More importantly, development problems should not be used as an excuse to reduce public welfare.

On conclusion, I believe that improvment to any country itself social welfare, it can impact the country itself economy growth or recession significantly. Thus, any country needs to concern how to improve itself social welfare in order to improve economy growth, instead of improvement social poor problems for our future generation.

World needs keep peace

One important issue that human must need to concern if we hope our future societies can develop or improve in success. This issue is that " our world must need to keep peace. Why and how our word must need to keep peace ? The reason is very simple. If our future countries aim to only to be the world top leader, every leader only concentrates on finding the best method to become world top leader, he/she neglects to concern how to make himself/herself country to develop technology, medicine, construction, social welfare etc. different social aspect issues. His/her time only concentrates on war aspect, so peace world is the major key to help our next generation can have safe, clean and good economy social environment to work and live in our world anywhere. The question is : How to keep peace world to avoid war? Ambitious leader must not respresent that he/she must be the top leader that he/she has effort to dominate any countries matter. He/she ought need to know peace is the most important factor that when every country can cooperate to do any matter in order to solve any social challenges, due to cooperation can help any country leader to reduce time to find the best solution when any county leader faces difficulties. So, leader cooperation must need to keep world peace in our future society, moreover, any country improvement must need any country leader cooperation to sit down to discuss any important issues together. It is the best method to build global the most safe society in order to let any country citizen to feel comfortable and safe to live in themselves countries.